ANTIQUES
for
AMATEURS
Secrets to Successful Antiquing

Milan Vesely

Published by

 **krause
publications**

700 E. State Street • Iola, WI 54990-0001

Please call or write for our free catalog. Our toll-free number to place an order
or obtain a free catalog is 800-258-0929 or please use our regular business
telephone 715-445-2214 for editorial comment and further information.

Library of Congress Catalog Number: 98-87286
ISBN: 0-87341-712-7
Printed in the United States of America

Table of Contents

Chapter One

Why Antiques?

"Who would prefer to live with cold stones when they could spend their day amid the warm glow of antique furniture created by men of genius" —*Judith Krantz*

"Who would prefer to live with cold stones when they could spend their days amid the warm glow of antique furniture created by men of genius?"

This passage from the writings of Judith Krantz best sums up how antique collectors feel about their chosen hobby. Passion, elation, frustration, and unbridled enthusiasm seem to fill the bosoms of growing legions of antique collectors and this interest is growing by leaps and bounds. Everywhere one looks there's something about antiques...on television, in newspaper columns, on the radio and even as a subject of conversation around the office water cooler. Who doesn't have a mother or a grandmother who has tons of them filling every nook and cranny of her home, or even a father-in-law who collects antique Civil War memorabilia?

But what constitutes an antique and how can you satisfy this curiosity you have about them? Where can you get honest-to-goodness useful information you can understand without having to wade through a lot of boring technical stuff?

Where do you start?

Libraries and bookstores aren't much help. Row upon row of books cover every conceivable antique in the greatest detail. Books on pottery, glassware, antique dolls and even movie memorabilia fill shelves as far as the eye can see. Not to mention the price guides: There are enough of them to sink the Titanic. Just to get a simple overall understanding of the antique business you're going to have to spend a fortune at Barnes and Noble or spend every free evening browsing your favorite corner bookstore's shelves.

Welcome to the real world. I understand your confusion. Like you, I am sometimes overwhelmed by all the information out there — and I'm an expert. Hence *Antiques for Amateurs: Secrets to Successful Antiquing.* Like my previous books, *Money From Antiques* and *More Money From Antiques,* this book is informative and fun to read. It's for people like you and me — ordinary people who just want to make sense out of a wonderful but increasingly complex subject. *Antiques For Amateurs* will give you all the information you need in one easy-to-read, condensed book. You will become knowledgeable without becoming bored. So, without further ado, let's get started.

Why antiques?

Most people become interested in antiques for one of two reasons. They either have an interest in collecting a particular type of antique purely for personal enjoyment (ceramics or pottery are the most common), or they start out curious about the antiques business as a whole without having anything specific in mind. But they all want to be sure of one thing — that what they buy will appreciate in value. That's what antiques are all about, isn't it? All those stories about people who buy some piece of junk at a garage sale that turns out to be a valuable antique worth thousands of dollars are really true, aren't they? And if they can do it, why can't you?

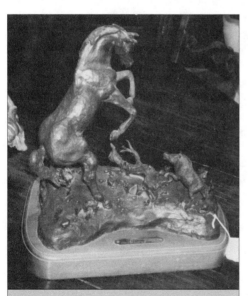

Most people want to be sure of one thing — that what they buy will appreciate in value.

Whatever the reason for your interest in antiques, two principles apply: know everything you can about the antiques that interest you, and obtain them at the lowest possible price. By doing so you will not only get maximum enjoyment out of owning the antique, but you'll also be sure that your investment appreciates in value over time.

So how do you do that?

By becoming knowledgeable in the main antique product categories, that's how. Not just knowledgeable, but also sufficiently confident in your own ability to ensure that you won't make a major mistake and lose a lot of money.

A word of caution here: *Antiques for Amateurs* will give you all the information you need to make good judgments and to hold your own when negotiating with any antique dealer. It will not, however, make you a specialist in all product lines, particularly the fringe ones such as Oriental antiques or Old Master paintings. For that you will need specialized knowledge obtained through a lot of research. *Antiques for Amateurs* will, however, give you sufficient knowledge so that you can confidently get involved in antiques for both pleasure and a bit of profit. For those readers interested in antiques as a business I also recommend you buy my books *Money from Antiques* and *More Money from Antiques* as these books cover the operations of an antique business and give you information outside the scope of this product guide.

What is an antique?

In today's modern world just about anything old is described as an antique and in generic terms that is true. In reality, antiques are products that are more than 100 years old or products that are sufficiently rare so as to put an intrinsic value on them. In other words, antiques are old products that are in limited supply. The more limited, the more antique the product.

Another way to think of antiques is as something collectible. Whether the product is furniture you want to collect to enhance the look of a room, a ceramic piece to decorate a corner cupboard, or some silverware you want to hand down to your grandchildren, the products are rare enough to be considered antiques. Everything else is secondhand goods or junk.

One misconception people have about antiques is that the older they look, the more antique it must be. Wrong! Appearance has nothing to do with it. Just because it looks like it came out of grandma's attic does not mean it is an antique. Not in the true sense of the word. If no one wants it, no matter how old it looks, it's just a piece of junk. Antiques have value, and that value is based on demand due to suitability and limited supply.

What kind of antique?

Anyone who has visited an antique mall with rows and rows of booths has probably felt like a pebble in a gravel pit. Hundreds and hundreds of products are everywhere. Furniture, ceramics, pictures, jewelry, old Coca-Cola signs and even products that look like the cat dragged them in. It all seems so confusing. And the prices for some products seem absolutely ludicrous! Particularly to the beginner. It's enough to make one give up before one's even started.

Don't worry. Like the new computer you bought with all those confusing software features, there's method to the madness of the antique business. It's just that the variety of products is so great that when you see them for the first time it seems as if every attic in town has been emptied and dumped into one building. Like computer software, however, it soon falls into place as you begin to classify the products into categories. Think of it like this: Like Windows 95 software there are main windows (categories) to cover everything. Within these are sub-windows (product lines) and within these there are even more subdivisions.

Antiques are a lot like Windows 95. All you need to know are the main categories. The sub-categories can take care of themselves until you need to know something specific about them, and when you do, all you have to do is isolate them and they fall into place on their own.

So what are these main categories?

Furniture, ceramics, glassware, silverware, commemorative items and toys are just a few of the main categories. All in all there are approximately fifteen major categories with probably seventy-five sub-categories. Within these there are other, more specialized areas. Antique maps and cigar collectibles, for instance, are good examples of two such specialized areas. Both of these have sprung up quite recently and both are still defining their own parameters.

My point is this: No real way to define categories exists, and therefore certain antique product lines have simply fallen into their own definitions. Therefore, antique dealers and enthusiasts refer to them in general terms, which are understood by the majority of the antique-interested public. I say all this so you'll understand that categorizing antiques is not important and that you should not feel hesitant if you don't know a particular term.

More important to serious antique dealers or enthusiasts is the historical periods covering various product lines. Victorian, Roman, Gothic, Civil War, Western and even '50s are terms used to age products. These terms are also used to indicate style. Victorian English means the time period associated with Queen Victoria's reign. Within this are pre-Prince Albert and after Albert's death periods. This change is signified first by a fancy and very decorative style, followed by a very somber, basic style. The reason for this is that prior to Prince Albert's death, English furniture makers took their cue from their Queen's mood. Desperately in love, she was extremely happy, hence the fancy and decorative pieces. After her consort's death her sadness was reflected in the furniture makers' pieces, which became rather stark and basic. Interesting, isn't it? Not only are we able to identify certain historical periods from antiques, but also the moods and attitudes prevalent at the time. That's what makes antiques such a fascinating business.

And it is a business

How do you buy a piece without paying through the nose? How can you ensure that you won't be taken to the cleaners? How does one make sense of all the confusion? Question upon question follows. That's where *Antiques for Amateurs* can help. It's a guidebook for beginners interested in getting an overview of the antiques business so they feel more comfortable. It is for the real-world antique person and not the rarefied expert of the Sotheby's or Christie's auction houses. It is also not written for museum experts who specialize in period pieces that interest only a select few people. It is for you and me — those who want an overall feel for the antique business to enable us to make rational decisions about what interests us.

Enough of the explanations. Let's take a look at some of the categories, shall we?

Porcelain: Porcelain antiques fall into categories associated with the country of manufacture. English, German, American, Spanish, Chinese and Japanese are just a few of these. The three main areas of interest are English, German and Chinese with American close behind. Names such as Royal Doulton, Staffordshire, and Meissen will soon become words you'll be familiar with. You'll learn about the Blue Willow pattern, which easily stands out as the most popular ceramic collected worldwide. Limoge, Belleek, and Sevres will also intrigue you, as will a whole host of other products in this very crowded category.

Furniture: English, French, American and Chinese are the four types you'll encounter in an antique mall or auction sale. English furniture is usually Victorian or pre-Victorian. American furniture tends to fall into types: Shaker; New York; or Western. Chinese furniture is often referred to by the period of manufacture.

Glassware: English, Continental and Venetian are the three terms most used. Bohemian is sometimes used to distinguish German or Czech glass. Dating becomes important with circa 1700 and 1800. Glassware collectors and dealers tend to specialize in a particular product line such as decanters, drinking glasses, bowls or jugs. Glassware is a very large antique category and immensely popular as most people can identify with its everyday use.

Silverware: Silverware is also a very popular antique collectible. Here again, English, German and American silverware predominates. Like glass, this category is defined by product type. Teapots, candlesticks, flatware and bowls are all highly sought after. Classification in this category is by make and markings generally stamped on the back of the products. Sterling and Sheffield silver are the two most recognizable types. EP is often seen as a marking and stands for silver Electro Plate. Sheffield silver is a combination of a layer of silver and copper beaten together to give a silver surface with a warm sheen.

Jewelry: Precious and semi-precious, as well as costume jewelry are the dominant categories with Victorian era jewelry (the most popular period). Specialized knowledge is required in the precious jewelry category, but most ordinary folks soon become familiar with the semi-precious stones and the costume jewelry found in all antique malls. Pins, earrings and bracelets are the most popular product lines.

Commemorative antiques: Relying mainly on English Royalty and history, the commemorative antique category consists of anything celebrating an occasion. Royal weddings, a monarch's reign, births and victorious battles are all occasions for producing commemorative products. The Victorian period is the most popular, but more localized events such as battles or achievements are also forever immortalized on plates, jugs and spoons.

Toys: Dolls, dolls, and more dolls dominate this category with teddy bears a close second. There are other products, but from a value standpoint, dolls and bears dominate. English and German dolls are most sought after while German Steiff bears are desired almost exclusively. This category generates more emotion among collectors than does any other. As a result, collectors and dealers become very competent and have extremely specialized knowledge. A beginner in antiques should tread lightly as this is a very technical category filled with passionate and very knowledgeable people.

Oriental: Another highly technical category best avoided by beginners, Chinese and Japanese antiques dominate this category. Eighteenth Century Tang, Quing, and Cantonese pieces are quite popular, and Japanese antiques are particularly sought after by Japanese collectors who tend to be very nationalistic. Imari ceramics and Satsuma pottery are much in demand among this group of wonderful antique buffs.

Clocks, Barometers and Instruments: This is a very popular general category particularly among men. English, French and Austrian clocks dominate. In the "Longcase," or pendulum grandfather clocks, the English manufacturers stand out with

The beauty of a clock.

the value of the clock being as much in the beauty of the cabinetry as in the mechanical workings. A beginner should get familiar with names such as Thomas Field, McCabe, and Japy Freres. Like the doll category, antique collectors and dealers of clocks are very knowledgeable on individual makes. In the barometer category, chronometers are the ones to know about, particularly marine chronometers. These seem to invoke the smell of the sea in their aficionados who may even get a dreamy look when discussing their favorite piece. Again, English makers predominate. Among instruments, telescopes are popular as are surveying instruments. Microscopes and medical instruments follow hard on their heels.

Memorabilia: This category is dominated by Walt Disney products, particularly those to do with classics such as "Snow White." Musical memorabilia is also popular with Elvis memorabilia standing head and shoulders above other items. Postcards, Coca-Cola signs and signed autographed copies of correspondence are also in demand. This is a fun category as it's so diverse. It does, however, need time to absorb its particular idiosyncrasies. It is also very fickle and tends to go through fashion periods when prices fluctuate widely.

Militaria: This category is easy to type, isn't it? The title speaks for itself. Arms and armor, swords and daggers, pistols, revolvers and medals with a few military headdresses thrown in, sums up this category. British, German, American and Italian items are all covered in this class. For the beginner it is best to avoid these antiques until you have time to study them. Definitely a man's "thing," military antiques cover everything related to wars and regimental history.

Collectibles: A very large category of antiques, collectibles cover everything from blue willow patterned ceramics, which are popular with women, to the war medals popular with men. Just remember what a collectible is. It is a limited supply antique gathered or accumulated for pleasure or as a hobby. A very trendy category, collectibles nevertheless have basic product lines, such as ceramic plates, perfume bottles, pocket watches, stamps, and even figurines that continue to grow year after year. My advice on collectible antiques is to ask around to find out what is currently hot. Add this product line to the basic ones mentioned above and you can't go wrong.

Architectural antiques: This is a new antique category that is very much in vogue and appears to be gathering strength. Covering wrought iron, pedestals, statues, water fountains, fire surrounds, garden furniture and finials, among other items, architectural antiques are mainly of English and Italian manufacture of 19th century vintage. For a beginner this is an exciting category because one can very quickly become an expert since there are so few around. Architectural antiques are also fun as they are now being used extensively for both interior and exterior decoration. What's more, they are skyrocketing in price and will continue to do so in the foreseeable future.

Miscellaneous antiques: Anything fits under this category! Tribal wood carvings, leather furniture, Art Nouveau, marble, metalware — any material will do. For the antique beginner I have this advice: If it's old — preferably very, very old — and looks gnarly, unusual and even ugly, it is a good antique to take an interest in — as long as you buy it for a song! After all, you can always use it as a door stop.

As you can see from the above categories, there are some glaring omissions. This is deliberate. Pictures and paintings are one of the obvious missing categories. Why? *Antiques for Amateurs* is the title of this book and, as such, I have deliberately ignored paintings because a beginner should not even consider buying or selling these items due to their technical nature and extremely high prices. Russian works of art are another category left out for the same reason. The same can be said of Islamic antiques, antique carpets and bronzes. That is not to say that you shouldn't look at these product categories. Just don't go spending large sums of money hoping you'll get a bargain. Too many specialists have already been there before you.

I will, however, cover these categories in some detail toward the end of the book for those who have a hankering for living dangerously!

The other reason that I left out some categories is that they are relatively rare. They are on the fringe of the antique business. For instance, transport vehicles such as antique bicycles, canoes and wagons are antiques in their own right, but are seldom seen in the fascinating everyday world of antiques. But I will cover each of the major categories in detail in their respective chapters. Once we have done so you will be able to hold your own with any antique dealer you may encounter when buying and selling antiques. My intention is that by reading this book you will gain a good overview of the business as a whole and you'll feel confident when discussing various product lines. I might add that if you remember even half of what's in this book you will be more of an expert than 80 percent of the so-called dealers one will come across in any mall.

Advice: Antiques fall into two categories — the real-world one, and the rarefied one that most people can only ooh and aah at. This book deals with *Antiques for Amateurs*

Browsing through antique malls as much as possible will help.

and so I shall stick to the former. Not only is this level of antiques more fun but it is also the level at which most people can get involved.

Another piece of advice: Try to learn just the main product names at first. Delft, Blue Willow, Victorian and Staffordshire will take you a long way in the real world of ceramic antiques. Periods are also important. Late 17th century, 19th century and even early '50s is the language that most antique enthusiasts know. Don't rush to learn everything at once as you will pick these up pretty quickly. Browsing through antique malls as much as possible will help. You will be surprised how much you can pick up just by reading labels. Associating styles with descriptions will also bring your knowledge up to speed extremely quickly. A Saturday afternoon spent browsing will be invaluable. It will bring what I have written to life.

But how much should you spend when you do locate the perfect piece?

Prices are a confusing issue for the antique beginner. This is such an important aspect for the beginner that I am going to stick my neck out and give you some hard and fast guidelines to remember.

At a good auction this should fetch $10,000 to $15,000.

1. Treat all prices as inflated. Antiques are such subjective items that prices vary tremendously depending on demand, current trends, and rarity. I always chuckle when I hear appraisers on a popular TV show quote the value of an item they are appraising. "At a good auction this should fetch $10,000 to $15,000," they say to gasps of amazement from the owner. Sure! Is it $10,000 or is it $15,000? The difference is huge to me. One other factor: just try to sell that piece to them. That's when you'll really find out what the real value is. Half of the $10,000 is more likely what you will be offered, if not less.

2. Buying is always easier than selling. Remember that rule when making an offer on an antique. Offer? Yes. You heard me correctly.

Always make an offer on antiques. Being so subjective, your assessment of value is as good as the next person's. Never take the price advertised as final — make an offer!
3. Antiques appreciate over the long term. Like the stock market, antiques rise and fall in value depending on demand, the trend, or simply the effects of El Ninõ. If you're purchasing as an investment rather than purely for pleasure bear this in mind: Buy low, sell high. It's even more important with antiques because valuation is so subjective.

But don't let me scare you off. Antiques have a lot to offer.

Antiques are tremendously satisfying items to be involved with. Their history alone is fascinating. As a window to the past, antiques allow us the privilege of witnessing the world as it was before technology smothered everything with its speed and blandness. Just studying the artist's brush strokes on a commemorative, hand-painted Royal Doulton plate gives us an insight into his or her thinking. Isn't that wonderful? Did that upward curl indicate that the lady or gentleman was happily looking forward to a celebratory evening with his or her loved one in 1720? And did the flourish at the end of that grapevine the artist painted the next day indicate how much fun and how satisfying it was? Use your imagination.

Fun, isn't it?

The entire world of antiques lies before us. It's filled with wonderful stories, objects of art and fascinating history. Not to mention money. Let's go explore it, shall we?

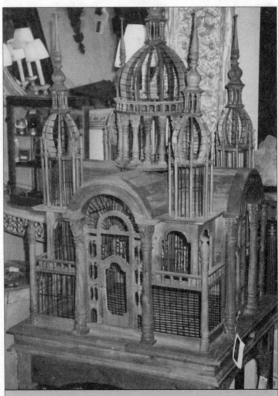

The world of antiques is filled with wonderful objects.

Chapter Two

Pottery, Porcelain, Ceramics and Others

Porcelain items are the most popular antiques collected by enthusiasts.

Porcelain and ceramic items are probably the most popular antiques collected by enthusiasts and traded by dealers. Only accessory furniture comes anywhere close. The reasons for this are many, but the fact that porcelain antiques are attractive display items is a major factor. From figurines to fruit bowls, wall plates and vases, everyone likes their home to look pretty, and porcelain products certainly do that. Not only do they look pretty, but they have an interesting history.

Before going into detail on the various manufacturers of antique pottery, I want to explain what the various descriptive words mean that relate to this category. Porcelain, ceramic, stoneware and even bone china are used by people who are not often sure of what the differences are. As an antiques beginner, knowing the meaning of these terms will be of tremendous help.

All cups, plates, jugs, and pots can be considered "pottery."

Glaze is a liquid combination of glass forming minerals combined with stiffeners and melting agents.

All cups, plates, jugs and pots can be considered pottery. In other words, any clay that is chemically altered and hardened by firing in a kiln. The type of pottery or ceramic is determined by the clay's composition, how it is prepared, what kind of glazes are used (lead or glass) and the firing temperature. Variations in this process give us the following:

Earthenware: A porous pottery fired at the lowest kiln temperatures. Depending on the clay used (normally associated with the area in which the pottery is made), earthenware turns a buff, red, brown or black color when fired. It often looks like a handicraft item rather than a professionally manufactured item, which is not strictly true.

Stoneware: Water resistant and much more durable, a stoneware clay mix turns white, buff, gray, or red when fired at higher temperatures and it's usually glazed.

Porcelain: Porcelain is made from a decomposed, granite clay called Kaolin and is white or translucent. It was first made in China, hence its common name, china.

Bone china: Invented in the mid-18th century, bone china came about when English potters added powdered, chemically altered ox bones to the clay to give it a harder consistency. It also added whiteness, translucency, and stability. Because of its hardness, bone china items were of a thinner composition.

Colors are obtained from metal oxides.

Blue onion patterns used cobalt blue coloring.

Glaze: Glaze is a liquid combination of glass-forming minerals combined with stiffeners and melting agents. When melted, the mix becomes glass-like at temperatures suited to the clay compositions. The effects of glazes on specific clays depend on the clay's composition and on the potter's skill in controlling the glaze firing (melting and hardening). Salt glazes, creamware (lead glaze with calcined flint), and blue-tinted creamware (Wedgewood) are all variations of glaze mixtures applied to specific clay compositions.

Colors: Colors can be obtained from metal oxides, tins, enamels, or they can come from designs printed on paper and transferred to the item while wet. When transferring patterns, the transfer paper gets burned away in the firing leaving the colored design behind. Hand-painted enamels or oxides give great value to a piece because of the skill and labor required to apply them.

Mastering the descriptions above will immediately make you competent in assessing an antique pottery piece. Just remember that variations in these characteristics were experimented with in Japan, East Asia, the Middle East and China. The best way to get comfortable with identifying specific pieces is to practice doing so, then check to see if you were right.

In the real day-to-day world of antiques, porcelain antiques are classified by manufacturer with German and English makers predominating. French and Italian are also popular. Belleek Irish porcelain is gathering strength as are Song and Tang Dynasty Chinese ceramics followed by Japanese Imari and Arita products. As a beginner in antiques it is essential that you know the main manufacturers and some details about their strong periods. Here they are:

Meissen: The most important of all manufacturers and located in southeast Germany on the river Elbe, the Meissen factory was established in 1710. Developed by ceramist Johan Friedrich Bottinger, Meissen ceramics were known for their hard-paste porcelain and their very high level of decoration. Hand painting is their specialty and hence the reason for antique Meissen ceramics' increasingly high prices. Exquisite detail is also a hallmark of Meissen ceramics whose spectrum of products covers everything from single cups to large compotes (long stemmed fruit bowls). Meissen is particularly famous for its Blue Onion pattern, which represents symbols of East Asian culture with pomegranate, peach, bamboo, lotus flower and chrysanthemum designs.

Antique beginners should look for the Blue Onion patterns that used cobalt blue, a particularly heat-resistant paint. Crossed sword markings with the word Meissen in scrolled letters identify a genuine Meissen piece. Kakiemon Meissen designs manufactured around 1730 look very oriental and fetch high prices.

Recommendation: An antique beginner cannot go wrong with genuine Meissen ceramics which will continue to increase in price. You can recognize them by the intricate figurines, the attention to detail, hand painting, the oriental designs with cobalt blue colors, and crossed sword markings with scrolled Meissen lettering.

Royal Worcester: Founded in 1751 in Worcester, England, by physician Dr. John Wall, production of Royal Worcester continues in the same town yet today. Their products consist of ornamental ceramics, tiles, dining sets, tea sets, kettle handles, plates and much more. Extremely decorative, the 1751 to 1783 'Dr. Wall' pieces are the ones to seek; however, all Worcester's highly resistant-to-thermal-shock, soaprock pieces are good buys. Worcester porcelain is distinguishable by its bright colors, fine detail, and an "Orange Band" pattern around the edges. Most pieces are signed on the back and antique pieces by artists Chamberlain, Freeman and Ayerton are sought after.

Antique beginners can't go wrong with Worcester porcelain pieces, which are generally of modest price. Complete tea and dining sets are the products of choice. Try to find the hand-painted pieces rather than the transfer printed ones although early transfer ones are good value. Check that pieces have the Worcester marking on the back and are signed by the artist.

Recommendation: Worcester porcelain is a great way for an antiques beginner to get introduced to ceramics because of its reasonable price, wide variety, and increasing value. Buy signed pieces as an investment. You can't go wrong.

Limoges: Who hasn't heard of French Limoges? Started by Leon Sazaret in the 1850s, Limoges porcelain is a hard-paste Kaolin and feldspar porcelain obtained around Limoges, 200 miles south of Paris in the Haute Vienna region. The style of the early Limoges consisted of gold designs, and themes of flowers or people. Their table china in particular was decorated in a delicate style with gold trim as its second most definitive characteristic. Referred to as "Gold Coin," it was used frequently on table china manufactured from 1870 to the 1920s. After 1891 the name "France" was added to the mark and the notation "Mark 1" on white ware was also included after Sazaret's death in 1891.

Genuine Limoges antiques are relatively rare, unlike Worcester, and therefore an expensive way for the antiques beginner to start collecting. Dark blue vases with gold trim are a good buy if found. Transfers were used on table china, which is more readily available, but the general shortage of genuine Limoges antiques keeps prices high.

Recommendation: An antique beginner should exercise care with Limoges porcelain as it is rare to find genuine bargains. If you are in Europe on vacation you have a better chance of finding value-for-money items. Some pieces are also advertised on the Internet. As recommended in my books *Money From Antiques* and *More Money from Antiques,* always make an offer, no matter how you are buying.

Royal Doulton: In 1815, on the eve of the Battle of Waterloo, potter John Doulton was taken into partnership by Martha Jones, a widow who had inherited a pottery in Vauxhall Walk, Lambeth, by the side of the river Thames in South London. With her foreman, they formed Jones, Watts and Doulton, manufacturers of vitrified stoneware of the highest degree of perfection. Carried on by Doulton's son Henry, who was later knighted by Queen Victoria, Royal Doulton became famous for bone china and the on-glaze enamel decoration of their colorful faience, maiolica (spelled like this by experts) and delft wares. Through the talents of the brilliant, Victorian period-trained artists like Joseph Hancock, Henry Tittensor, Edward Birks and Percy Curnock, Royal Doulton perfected the much sought after color effects of the ancient Chinese Sung and Chung wares. They also achieved the Rouge Flambe color effects on figures and character jugs, which reflected the moods and fantasies of the world around them, and a vast array of on-glazed enamel Bone China products.

Royal Doulton products are ideal for collecting. All of high quality, their wall plaques, vases, and character figurines are relatively plentiful, and the company introduced its products into the United States as early as 1901 at exhibitions in Chicago. Early 1800s Royal Doulton pieces signed by one of their many renowned artists are still available in the antiques market. Buy them if you can.

Recommendations: Synonymous with Fine Bone China, Royal Doulton pottery is an ideal way for an antiques beginner to wet their feet in antique ceramic collecting. There is a wide range of products that are both affordable and interesting. Specialize in character figurines, fine Bone China sets or the simple "simplicity" plaques or vases manufactured in the between-wars period. Many 1900 pieces are an excellent value since once they get through the 100-year genuine antique dating period their prices skyrocket. If you can find an original Lambeth Doulton piece snap it up and celebrate. You have just hit the jackpot!

Basket weave latticework.

Belleek: "When Irish eyes are smiling . . .!" Lovely song, isn't it?

Founded in 1857 in Belleek village, County Fermanagh, Northern Ireland, this Irish pottery is enjoying popularity as a collectible among antique dealers and collectors alike. Abundant quantities of feldspar and other raw materials around the picturesque village ensured a high level of quality. Belleek pottery is renowned for its three-strand and basket weave latticework which makes it easily recognizable. Early 1800s pieces are now pricey but late-1800 items are still reasonable and will increase in value dramatically. Belleek pottery is marked and easy to date, although confusing. The period 1863-1890 was marked with a wolfhound's head turned to face a tower to the right of what is an Irish harp. Two sprigs of shamrock border the black Belleek banner below. In the 1891-1926 period the words "Co. Fermanagh, Ireland" were added and between 1926-1946 the words "Deanta in Eirinn" (made in Ireland) were also included.

Belleek baskets are the products a beginner needs to collect, although these are hard to find. Ensure that the weave is in good condition. As with all delicate ceramic strands these tend to get broken frequently. Other Belleek earthenware products are not as popular, although taking a chance on them increasing in value dramatically may be worth the risk.

Recommendation: Belleek baskets are well worth collecting for an antiques beginner, especially if the price is right. The wolfhead and tower marked ones should not be passed over. As a second string to Meissen collecting, Belleek baskets are not just extremely pretty but also a good investment for the antiques beginner.

Sevres: Expensive Sevres porcelain was originally made in Vincennes but transferred to Sevres, France, in 1756. Three years later King Louis XV became the principle shareholder and the factory was designated the "Royal Porcelain Manufactory." Thereafter it manufactured luxury porcelain mainly for the French royal family, the French court, and the large French aristocracy. It continues to do this today. In 1760 deposits of kaolin (china clay) were found in Limoges, France, which enabled Sevres to change from soft-paste porcelain to hard-paste manufacture. Unlike other manufacturers, Sevres porcelain was made by numerous artists collaborating in the painting and finish of the same piece and Sevres antiques usually have many personal identification marks incised into the paste or painted over the glaze. The factory's crossed L's enclosing a date letter are also always marked. "A" indicates 1753, "B" means 1754, and so on. When they exhausted the alphabet in 1777 they began using double letters (i.e. AA, BB, etc.). Hard-paste porcelain pieces had a crown added above the crossed L's.

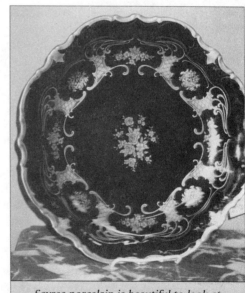

Sevres porcelain is expensive and they used gilt extensively. Like Meissen, their porcelain is top of the line and their plaques and pieces with Marie Antoinette and other French personalities fetch high prices. Antique soft-paste pieces fetch five-figure prices and are closely held on to. Beautiful to look at, and renowned for the richly colored backgrounds and white panels decorated with birds, Sevres is for wealthy antique collectors only.

Sevres porcelain is beautiful to look at.

Staffordshire was the porcelain center of England.

Recommendation: Sevres porcelain is too rich for the antique beginner but it is the type of porcelain that will win you the jackpot if you happen to strike it lucky in some musty old estate sale. Keep an eye out for the gilt, the heavier the better, as it may indicate a pearl among swine at an estate sale.

Staffordshire: The Staffordshire Pottery lasted from 1889 to 1948 when it was succeeded by the Crown Staffordshire Porcelain Company. Renowned for its famous people figurines as well as its whimsical animal pottery, Staffordshire antique pottery is probably the most widely collected of all porcelain due to its price, availability, and wide range of subjects. Its soldier figurines are prized by military buffs world-wide, and its child figures are the most widely collected porcelain of all time. It varies in price based on the availability of specific pieces, but Staffordshire porcelain enables the antique beginner to start at the lower level and work up to the more valued and harder-to-find pieces.

Staffordshire was the porcelain center of England in the 1800s and continues to be so today. As a result, Staffordshire is often referred to as porcelain from the Staffordshire area rather than from a specific manufacturer. Mainly concentrating on decorative figurines, animal clusters and other whimsical products, Staffordshire porcelain is moderately priced but varies in quality depending on manufacturer. It is an ideal antique ceramic for the beginning antique collector or dealer due to its widespread demand and reasonable prices.

Recommendation: Like Worcester porcelains, Staffordshire antiques are perfect for the antique beginner. Concentrate on collections rather than on a medley of different subjects. Choose something that is of interest to you — soldier figurines, animal pieces or whimsical moldings — and collect these. Remember that the value of individual pieces rises dramatically when they are part of a matching collection. Keep an eye out for rare Victorian era pieces such as religious items as these fetch double and triple prices. For example, a rare 1855 religious group is worth approximately $6,000 while the more available and ordinary figurines are worth only around $500. Condition is also vital in Staffordshire porcelain as damaged pieces appreciate less than perfect pieces.

Notation: From here on out I shall quote prices. These should be taken purely as a guide. Antique prices go up and down and it is difficult to be specific or very accurate when things change so much. I am sticking my neck out and quoting prices, however, as I feel that too often a beginner doesn't even have a sense of what a particular antique is worth. I hope that this will be of help to everyone. Besides, I like living dangerously.

Summary: The manufacturers detailed above are the main producers of antique ceramics and their products are all highly collectible. For the beginner, antique ceramics from Meissen, Royal Worcester, Doulton and Staffordshire are the ones to concentrate on. Early 1800s manufactured products that are properly marked and signed by artists are good buys and are sure to appreciate in value. Sevres and Limoges products are in serious demand and if found at reasonable prices should be treated as a good investment. More second tier manufacturers are covered later in this chapter when I discuss Dresden, Crown Derby and Minton, among others.

Oriental Ceramics

Chinese and Japanese ceramics fascinate antique beginners, as does the Orient as a whole. For a change of pace I will discuss these in brief detail so that you as an antiques beginner have an educated overview. I'd like to reiterate that oriental antiques require specialized knowledge before you buy, since unlike European antique ceramics, Chinese pieces are considerably more difficult to identify and value. They are also in short supply with many reproductions flooding the market.

Chinese Ceramics: Chinese antiques, unlike European ones, are identified by dynasties and marks indicating short periods within those dynasties. The later Ming and Quing (Ch'ing) Dynasties are the best known but over seventeen dynasties cover the period between 1027 B.C. to 1368 A.D. The Ming dynasty covers the period 1368 A.D. to 1644 A.D. and the Quing the period 1644 to 1916.

Within the above dynasties there are identifiable periods such as the Jiajing (1522-1566), Guangxu (1875-1908) and Shunzi (1644-1661) periods. It is through these complex markings that Chinese antiques can be dated. Unless you are an expert, they are best left alone until you have become more confident and have studied them in detail. My recommendation is that you purchase a book with these periods detailed that you carry with you whenever buying Chinese antique ceramics.

Chinese and Japanese ceramics fascinate antique beginners.

Chinese porcelain was manufactured in many regions, but that from the Canton, Ching te Chen and Kiangsi Province are the best known. Shipped via Nanking Port on the lower Yangtze River in the 18th century, the bulk of Chinese export porcelain was the now well-known blue and white commonly called "Nanking." Often described as famille (meaning "of the family"), Chinese bowls, dishes, vases, cockerels, horses and figurines are prized by antique collectors both in the United States and worldwide.

Japanese Ceramics: Most Japanese porcelain was manufactured around the town of Arita in the Hizen Province within eight miles of the port of Imari. Shipped to Nagasati for export to Europe the term "Imari" is used to describe the type of decoration on Arita wares, namely underglaze blue with on-glaze iron red and gold decoration.

Like Chinese porcelain, Japanese manufacturers' names are rarely used. The terms "Arita" and "Imari" indicate a Japanese origin, and 18th and 19th century dating is the main focus of valuation. Condition and decoration — the mainstays of antique ceramic valuation — also play important parts in assessing Japanese ceramic desirability.

Japanese antiques, like the Chinese, mainly consist of bowls, vases, chargers (shallow dishes), plates and figurines. Heavily and intricately decorated with enamel painted flowers, trees, dragons and landscapes, Japanese porcelain commands a high price. Satsuma, a peninsula of Southwest Kyusha, also produced many flower and foliage decorated products featuring gilt bronze finishes.

Recommendation: As mentioned, Chinese and Japanese porcelains are fascinating, complex, and difficult product lines for the antique beginner to collect. If you wish to do so, I would recommend you buy yourself as many specialist books as possible and study the markings extensively. In short supply, oriental ceramics have been subjected to extensive faking and it takes an expert to distinguish the real thing. Because of this you could lose a lot of money if you are not extremely careful. Just remember the old adage: "If it sounds to good too be true, it probably is."

Other European Porcelain Manufacturers

Having digressed to the East I shall now cover the second tier of European manufacturers whose antique ceramics are often found in antique auctions, malls, and in the lengthy "For Sale" columns in newspapers. Here they are:

Royal Crown Derby: Founded by Huguenot Andrew Planche in Derby, England, sometime around 1740, this renowned potter was joined by William Duesbury and a group of extremely talented artists when they acquired the famous Chelsea China Works and Bow molds in 1770. Recognized for their lavishly decorated ceramics, they were granted the rare honor of being allowed to incorporate the crown in their backstamp by King George III. In 1890, Crown Derby was granted the seal of approval and given the title "The Royal Crown Derby Porcelain Company" by Queen Victoria. Exceptional flower paintings by artists Withers, Billingsly and Pegg, and landscapes by genius Boreman are the hallmarks of the 1786-1795 Royal Crown Derby period. For antique amateurs these pieces are a true find.

Rich colors and intricate gilding are the distinguishing features of Royal Crown Derby pottery. The tremendous variety of objects — all lavishly decorated — are what makes Crown Derby products highly collectible. Their aesthetic and functional pieces are an antique collector's delight. Concentrate on one line rather than collecting a hodgepodge of the many product types and you can't go wrong.

Recommendation: Antique beginners should concentrate on Crown Derby animal figures as their unusual decorations make them stand out among the myriad of ceramics available. Also highly desirable are their larger sized 1820s "Imri" Japanese style butter dishes. Crown Derby products are ideal for the beginner in the United States as they are relatively scarce and still mid-priced. They are sure to appreciate at an above-average rate as the burgeoning antique business discovers them. Of course by then you'll have a whole roomful, won't you?

Royal Crown Derby is recognized for its lavish decorations.

Royal Dux Bohemia: A real "sleeper," Royal Dux porcelain is an antique beginner's dream. Most people don't even know of this Czech Republic manufacturer, let alone recognize the value of its products. In 1709, German Johann Friedrich Bottger managed to break the thousand-year-old Chinese porcelain secrets and porcelain production developed across Europe rapidly until, in 1853, it reached Duchcov (Dux), located north of Prague in the Czech Bohemia area. Early production of majolica (Italian earthenware design) and faience (earthenware with colorful opaque glazes) quickly established Eduard Eichler's "Dux" factory at the forefront of ceramic production. History then played its tricks and in 1948 the communists nationalized the factory, resulting in its demise. Re-privatized in 1990 after a period of over 42 years, the factory is now rising to its pre-Cold War prominence.

Royal Dux figurines are highly prized in Europe and fetch really high prices. Delicate, extremely realistic and detailed in exquisite colors, Royal Dux is rising rapidly in the antique ceramic collectible world. For a beginner they are ideal products if they can be obtained because they are sure to appreciate considerably over the next decade. Just don't wait too long, they're already fairly pricey.

Recommendation: Buy any Royal Dux ceramics you can find and hold onto them for a few years. Take a trip to Europe if necessary. If you find any Royal Dux going cheap that you don't want, give me a call.

Coalport: Taking its name from the East Shropshire region of England, the John Rose Company is synonymous with Coalport ceramics and covers the period 1795 to 1926. Coalport ceramics are renowned for their boat-shaped tea pots and service sets and are very popular in England. Also sought after are their late 1800s English or Scottish scene pieces with gilt rococo decoration. J. Oldfield, A. Perry, and P. Simpson are artists recognized for their skill in depicting various Scottish Lochs on their sought after plates.

Coalport ceramics have a very limited demand in the United States but for an antique beginner they represent a bargain. If you find them, it will most likely be at "garage sale" prices. Sit on them for a few years or send them to England to cash out!

Recommendation: John Rose and Company Coalport ceramics are not suggested as an antique line for the beginner. You need more demand for your investment to appreciate substantially unless you are a risk taker, which I am.

Speaking of risks, the antique business is definitely a risky one. You have to be a bit of a gambler to be successful at it. Just don't pay too much for a piece and you can't really go wrong. You might have to sit on it for a few years but that's okay, isn't it? On the other hand, you just might find a gem and retire.

Spode: Joseph Spode I, 1733-1797, began manufacturing porcelain ornamented with Eastern art designs in Stoke-on-Trent, England, in 1784. His son, Josiah, later mixed kaolin feldspar with bone ash to make the harder "bone" China wares for which Spode is renowned. Their Regency style designs of the early 1800s are standouts and much sought after. Spode incorporates many blue and white pieces of sporting scenes in its production, and is well known for its collectibles as well as for its current variety of mid-priced ceramics. Their tea sets are coveted in Europe for their extensive decoration and gilt finish.

Spode antiques are mid-priced ceramics suitable for the antique beginner to collect. They're relatively rare, but can be found occasionally at reasonable prices. Watch for tea sets and blue and white patterns.

Recommendation: Spode antiques are relatively rare but because they're mid-priced, they are worth investing in for the long haul.

The antique pottery field is a crowded one.

Many other ceramics manufacturers have a collector following. Dresden, Chelsea, Lladro, Miles Mason, Capodumonti and Copeland among others. Each of them manufactured beautiful products that have their own following, but since this book is for the antique beginner, I have selected the top traded lines only.

Summary

The antique pottery field is a crowded one with many outstanding manufacturers. For the antique beginner, ceramics offer a relatively inexpensive and safe way to get involved because of the considerable market that exists for these products. My suggestion is that you settle on the price range that you feel comfortable with (i.e. Staffordshire, Royal Doulton or Royal Worcester for lower to mid range, Meissen for upper range, and Sevres or Limoges for the expensive range), and collect items that are part of a line. For those more adventurous, I recommend Royal Dux

Condition is everything.

Bohemia although these will take considerably more effort to find. You might consider combining a buying and vacation trip to Europe for this.

Here are some guidelines when buying ceramics:

1. Condition is vital. If repaired, make sure the repair is as invisible as possible. Damage can knock as much as 50 percent off the value of a piece.
2. Markings are essential. Look for the artist's signature and other indications of date of manufacture.
3. Never pay more than market value. Don't forget that retail is a 100 percent markup at least and the bigger discount you get, the better.

As we close out this chapter, I am mindful of how confusing many antique terms were to me as a beginner many years ago. With that in mind, here are a basic few that will enable you to hold your own in a conversation with any antique dealer or enthusiast. You never know, you might even find that you know more than most of them do.

Majolica (Maiolica): Is tin-glazed earthenware often richly decorated and colored similar to a type originally made in Italy. It is distinguished by its boldness rather than by finesse. The word Majolica is used by many other manufacturers who were situated nowhere near Italy to indicate bright, bold colors and a bold style of painting.

Delft: A style of blue and white glaze earthenware originally made in Delft, Netherlands. Later used by manufacturers to indicate both the blue and white and colored designs of the same style.

Blue Willow: Blue and white glaze designs of birds, pagodas, bridges and willow trees originally used by the Chinese but later reproduced by many European manufacturers. Make sure the design telling the story has three figures in it to be a true blue willow pattern.

Blue Willow originally came from China.

Chinoiserie: A style in art reflecting Chinese decorative and intricate patterns.

Earthenware: Pottery fired at the lowest temperature. Often buff, brown or red in color, earthenware has almost a handicraft-type appearance.

Stoneware: Water resistant and much more durable pottery that was fired at a higher temperature. Often gray or buff in color.

Porcelain: Made from a decomposed granite called kaolin, it is white or translucent in color.

Bone China: A hard porcelain originally discovered when English potters introduced ground bone to kaolin for strength. When flicked with a fingernail it produces a solid sound.

Provenance: The recorded history of an antique. Used more in furniture than with antique ceramics, it is always important if obtainable.

In concluding this chapter I have some practical suggestions for the antique beginner. However, I caution you that personal preference comes into everything. Still, my successful years in the antique business have given me an insight into ceramic products that are constantly in demand and therefore increasingly going up in value. Here are some recommendations for the antique amateur to start with.

Blue Willow Pattern: Collect these pieces. Their following is so huge that demand will continue to drive prices up. Beware of imitations that are flooding the market. Genuine pieces are increasingly hard to find but still appear in little-advertised estate sales.

Staffordshire Figurines: These also have a huge following, which gives the antique beginner security of investment. Concentrate on one type such as dogs, birds, or figures rather than mixing a whole hodgepodge of different types.

Collect blue willow — the following is huge!

Blue Willow and rare English delft.

Toby Jugs: Toby jugs manufactured by Wilkinson Ltd, Royal Doulton, Royal Worcester, Staffordshire, Prattware and Minton exhibit many strengths. Their advantage is that they are easily recognizable and that detailed information on desirability of certain jugs and their prices is widely available. A good men's collectible.

Antiques for Amateurs is the title of this book with the subtitle *Secrets to Successful Antiquing.* In view of this, here is a specialist's recommendation on ceramic products with some guideline prices.

> $1,500 and Under — Sevres and Meissen teawares, Delft plates, Derby figures and English enamel boxes are all good investments.

> $1,500 to $5,000 — Pre-1760 Worcester and Chelsea figurines with smaller Meissen and Royal Dux items are good value.

> $5,000 and above — Early Worcester, rare English Delft, complete antique dinner sets and porcelain snuff boxes are the hot ticket.

That was a lot to absorb, wasn't it? Don't worry, I started with pottery and ceramics for that very reason. Widely collected, bought and sold, ceramics are the heart and soul of the antiques business and as such, an antique beginner should know the basics, which I have detailed. Believe me, life will become a lot easier if you have absorbed even 20 percent of this chapter. By no means complete, it will make you competent and able to hold your own on antique pottery.

Lets move on to antique furniture, shall we?

Chapter Three

Furniture

Solid, hand-carved, historical furniture is a dying art.

Antique furniture's popularity is on an upward curve simply because it's an expression of one's character, a decoration in one's home, and an item of investment. The reason for this is simple: Solid wood, hand-carved, historical furniture is a dying art. Men are no longer creators; they are just computer operators, and time is at a premium.

For the beginner interested in antique furniture the old maxim still holds true: "Buy what you like and can live with, buy the very best you can afford, buy from reputable dealers with experience, and if you do all these things your investment will continue to appreciate."

Wood type is a significant value factor in antique furniture.

As with all antiques, condition determines value.

Like ceramics, antique furniture covers a vast range of types, designs, historical periods and styles. American, English, Continental (German and French) and Far Eastern furniture all have their following, and within each of these classifications are sub-classifications indicating both style and historical period. For all practical purposes, however, antique furniture can be considered as English, European, American and Chinese. Of these, the most important — both in price and by sales activity — is English furniture.

Wood type is a significant value factor in antique furniture, and mahogany, walnut, oak and pine predominate. Type of furniture, practicality, hardware and construction details are also important in determining value as is the originality of all the composite parts. Many pieces of antique furniture have replacement panels or have had hardware added due to breakage and this lowers the value of a piece drastically. One other factor should be considered. Many owners of antique furniture use lemon oil under the misguided belief that it helps preserve the wood and therefore enhances its value. This is an incorrect assumption. All it does is dry out the wood, darken the patina, and decrease its value. Make sure that only pure beeswax has been used on any piece you purchase. You can always tell if lemon oil has been used by the oily film left on your hand after rubbing the wood.

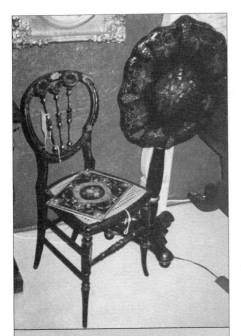

For the beginner, antique furniture provides fascinating insight into history.

Style is an indication of period as well as the wood used.

Antique furniture is hand-carved and special.

The more decorative Victorian styles.

As with all antiques, condition determines value. The better the condition, the higher the value. Slightly loose dove joints do not detract from the value of an antique piece, rather they indicate originality. Size also plays a part in value with smaller, rarer pieces fetching much higher prices than large, more common items. This is due to the diminishing size of modern homes and the resulting lack of space.

For the antique beginner, antique furniture offers fascinating insight into history. Unlike some other antiques, furniture styles instantly indicate periods. Early Victorian, for example, is instantly recognizable by its ornateness and the deep patina of the mahogany wood that was used so often. American Shaker stands out for its stark austereness and Chinese intricacy immediately identifies it as oriental. Bearing these basics in mind, here are the major styles and periods relevant to the real world of antique furniture. Before we discuss these here are a few words of advice on dating antique furniture.

Dating antique furniture is essential but this is both difficult and haphazard. Style is an indication of period as is the wood used. To be really sure however, the provenance of an antique furniture piece is vital, especially when purchasing expensive pieces. An antique beginner should resist spending large sums on a piece without obtaining a well documented provenance that can be verified.

English Antique Furniture

English antique furniture falls into Early English, Restoration, Georgian, Regency and Victorian periods. Each of these are distinct styles and easily identifiable. Manufacturers during these periods used English oak as the predominant wood but mahogany was prevalent in the early Victorian period.

Early English: Covering the reigns of Elizabeth I, James I, and Charles I during the period of 1558 to 1649, Early English furniture is also referred to as Elizabethan, Jacobean and Carolean furniture. Antique beginners need only remember it as Early English and that it has a solid, plain appearance with minimal decoration. Chairs in particular have a very upright appearance, although slightly decorative skirts were added to break up the overall starkness. With its plain, solid look, Early English antique furniture hasn't been as popular as the more decorative Regency and Victorian styles, although it's still worth buying for the mere fact its price increases steadily with age. Oak was the wood of choice during this period.

Recommendation: The antique beginner will have difficulty finding Early English furniture and should avoid buying replicas.

Restoration Furniture: Covering the period 1649 to 1714, this furniture is also referred to by experts as Cromwellian, Restoration, William and Mary, or Queen Anne. Beginners need only remember it as Restoration, since this period is not well known for its furniture pieces. Like Early English, the pieces are stark and basic. Another disadvantage is they are difficult to date. Decoration was used sparingly to break up the Germanic look. This is not a good period for the antique beginner to be involved in, although Queen Anne pieces are worth snapping up at bargain prices as they almost can be considered Georgian furniture. Oak again predominates.

Recommendation: As with Early English, Restoration furniture is not for the antique beginner.

A basic starkness offset by the use of mahogany, walnut, or beechwood.

Unusual pieces such as elbow chairs fetch high prices.

Georgian Period: Stretching through the reigns of George I, II, and III over the 1714 to 1812 period, Georgian furniture is a mid- to extremely high-priced antique period with the basic starkness offset by the mahogany, walnut and even birchwood that were used in its construction.

Thinner and more delicate wood thickness also distinguishes this period, particularly with chairs. Often recognized by the presence of decorative feet on relatively stark furniture pieces, Georgian furniture is much sought after and forms the backbone of the English antique furniture business. Unusual pieces such as dolphin chairs, elbow chairs, and serpentine commodes with fine patina, impeccable provenance (history), and good condition fetch high, six-figure prices. This alone renders them out of reach of most antique beginners. It should not, however, deter you from looking at Georgian furniture because reasonable pieces can still be found. When you consider the steadily climbing prices, these can be an excellent investment.

One cannot discuss the Georgian period without mentioning the name, Thomas Chippendale (1718-1779). For the antique beginner, Chippendale means furniture with flowing lines and rococo ornamentation as well as astronomically high prices. If you find a genuine piece of Chippendale furniture buried in some old barn at a price you can afford, you've struck it rich. Anything that even faintly resembles Chippendale furniture is worth buying on the off-chance that you could exchange it for a yacht in the Caribbean!

Recommendation: Georgian furniture is worth purchasing. For the antique beginner it offers both lower prices as well as astronomically priced pieces. This fact alone ensures that whatever you invest in will increase in value.

Distinguished by its ornateness, epitomized by Queen Victoria herself.

Stools, side tables, and more unusual items are popular.

Regency Furniture: From 1812 to 1830, Regency furniture was manufactured during the late reign of King George III and the reign of King George IV. Unlike the Georgian period, Regency furniture has never gained the fame or generated comparable demand. This may be due to anticipation of Queen Victoria's ascendance to the English throne. **Recommendation:** Regency furniture is reasonably priced and readily available, but is hard to distinguish from the Georgian furniture period. Sought more by decorators than by antique dealers, its products are not recommended for the antique beginner because the price appreciation is rather slow.

Victorian Furniture: Without a doubt the most glorious period in English furniture manufacture, Victorian furniture is an antique beginner's best friend. It's not as expensive as Georgian furniture, but it's popular and in demand, particularly in the United States. Many pieces can still be found at reasonable prices. Pieces are distinguished by their ornateness and delicate style, and they were manufactured in oak, mahogany, walnut and satinwood. Victorian furniture reflects an era of elegance and lightheartedness that Queen Victoria herself epitomized.

Victorian furniture, like all furniture, must be in good condition to appreciate in value. The mahogany pieces are more sought after and an antiques buyer should concentrate on these if possible. Stools, card tables, side tables and more unusual items like rolltop desks are the items an antiques beginner should try to find since they are popular as accent pieces in today's modern homes. Larger pieces, such as

French furniture represents the style and flair of kings.

German furniture is distinguished by its dark, heavy Gothic looks.

marble-topped tables with gilt legs, are much in demand along with cupboards, or linen presses as they are often called. Entertainment centers are also popular.

Recommendation: Victorian furniture is an ideal line for the antiques beginner. Whether they're purchased for investment or for one's own use, small accessory tables are good buys. If you're going to purchase English Victorian furniture for investment you should look for partners' desks, commodes (small clothes chests) or writing desks. Victorian dining table and chair sets are also good as they are in steady demand. Avoid pieces that are too flashy except for curio cupboards; and stay with mahogany, walnut and satinwood rather than oak. Welsh dressers are also always a great buy — the darker the better.

Continental Furniture

French: For the antique beginner French furniture represents the style and flair of Kings Louis XIV, XV, and XVI. Easily discernible due to its ornate marquetry and gilt and serpentine decoration, French furniture was made from exotic woods such as rosewood, kingwood and pearwood. French antiques are not as readily available as English furniture, and they're usually more expensive. French chairs stand out as items of beauty with their unique use of tapestry, needlework, or brocade. Walnut bedroom suites are another area where French ostentation excelled; these are in constant demand. Unlike other manufacturers, French artists often painted their creations, often in blue rococo style. Because they were close to northern Italy, French antique furniture makers used marble surfaces far more than English or German manufacturers and this is often the hallmark of the Louis XIV to XVI period, particularly on entry hall and bedside tables.

Recommendation: French antique furniture is not for the beginner. It's difficult to find in most regions of the U.S. Louisiana, Carolina, and Georgia are where the richness of French gilt, rococo and marble are most appreciated, while the Midwest considers it too garish.

German: German antique furniture is distinguished by its lack of availability and its dark, heavy, Gothic looks. Extremely heavily carved, often with ornate forest or hunting scenes, the dark and almost black Beidermeier furniture is in great demand by cognoscenti (people of superior taste or knowledge). German antiques can often be distinguished based on their use of unusual wood such as Hungarian ash, satinwood and walnut. German furniture rarely comes on to the market at prices a beginner should risk. Scottish furniture, which is almost the same in appearance, is a far better buy. This is also rising in price as the Germans snatch it up.

Recommendation: German antique furniture is not for the amateur, even if you could find it or afford it.

Italian: Italian antique furniture is the Cinderella of the pack. Italian antiques are extremely detailed and complex. The neoclassic styles stand out and they are very distinct in that they often have cabriole legs, gilt and are made of exotic woods such as beechwood. Much like French pieces, Italian 17th century manufacturers like to paint their creations and many used gilt extensively. Marble was the preferred material for top surfaces. Nude or semi-nude figures are often used as support features, and Italian antiques are scarce on the open market.

Dating and identifying manufacturers is difficult and requires specialized knowledge. If found, good Italian giltwood is usually priced in the five-figure bracket.

Recommendation: Although they're lovely to look at, Italian antiques are difficult for the amateur. If you like the human form, gilt, and can afford it, I would, however, recommend splurging. Your purchase is bound to be a good investment as rarity ensures increasing price.

Dutch: Almost indistinguishable from French furniture, Dutch furniture is rarely found in the U.S. and is usually in the form of chests of drawers or cupboards. This type of antique is too rare for an antiques amateur to bother with.

Recommendation: Ignore Dutch furniture and go for the English or French items instead.

Much like French pieces, Italian 17th century manufacturers liked to paint their creations.

Oriental furniture is almost totally limited to 19th century products.

Manufactured by immigrants, American furniture adopted its styles from the homelands of the craftsmen who made it.

Oriental Antiques

Oriental antique furniture is almost totally limited to 19th century Chinese products. Lacquered or inlaid folding screens, decorative occasional tables, and inlaid cabinets form the bulk of Chinese antiques and are much in demand. Inlaid with mother-of-pearl, ivory, bone, copper and brass, Chinese antiques are classified by dynasty period, much the same as Chinese ceramics. Surprisingly, they are reasonably priced considering their scarcity. Ming Dynasty (1368-1644) and Quing Dynasty (1644-1916) lacquered furniture is worth buying, but finding anything other than 19th century products would be extremely difficult.

Some Japanese antique furniture finds its way onto the U.S. market in the form of lacquered curio cabinets. These are popular and are always worth purchasing. Just make sure that it is a genuine piece by inspecting every nook and cranny to ensure that it looks old. If in doubt, pass up on the piece, as too many fakes abound.

Recommendation: Carved hardwood vase and flower stands as well as folding screens are what the antique beginner should concentrate on if interested in oriental antique furniture. Not a widely popular market, it nevertheless is an interesting one.

American Furniture

Manufactured by a nation of immigrants, American antique furniture adopted its styles from the homelands of the woodworking craftsmen who sought freedom in the New World. Much of the American furniture is therefore named after craftsmen, such as Hepplewhite, after European periods or designs such as Chippendale, or after religious or social movements, like Shaker. Here are a few of the better-known types and their specific characteristics:

Hepplewhite furniture is named after the late 1700s English cabinetmaker George Hepplewhite who published his clean-lined, well proportioned, and functional designs. Many of these were recreated by his countrymen in America.

Blanket chests are prized by collectors everywhere.

18th century Queen Anne furniture was reproduced in the United States to the same design as that manufactured by English furniture cabinetmakers during Queen Anne's 1702 to1714 reign.

18th and 19th century Pennsylvania furniture was a reproduction of German period designs. Pennsylvania German blanket chests are prized by antique collectors everywhere.

Pilgrim antique furniture took its name from the early 17th century pilgrims whose trials and tribulations were reflected in the stark functionality of their furniture pieces. They are manufactured from oak or ash and are difficult to find.

Shaker furniture, named after the 1747 English religious sect that observed celibacy while practicing communal living, was hand-crafted from Pennsylvania cherry wood. Rocking chairs designed and manufactured by Robert Wagan for the Mt. Lebanon, New York Shaker community in the 1860s are still in use today. Basic in design, with straight tapering legs, Shaker furniture is known for its clean lines and functional appearance.

Mission furniture (also called Stickly or Craftsman furniture) dates from around the turn of the century and is characterized by quality workmanship and simple, honest design. It's a style born of a social reform movement that emphasized the pride and dignity of the individual. Mission antiques are gaining in popularity, and Stickly, William Morris and Frank Lloyd Wright vintages are much sought after, but are probably too costly for the amateur antiquer.

Appalachian furniture is a recent addition to American antique furniture. Manufactured by the Appalachian mountain people, Appalachian furniture is very country-looking, straightforward in construction, and very strong and useful.

American antique furniture can be distinguished by the use of cherry wood, ash, and white oak in contrast to the European use of dark oak, mahogany and walnut.

A simple, honest design.

American antique furniture is gaining a strong following.

The majority of Americans are familiar with English furniture.

Auctioneers are able to get container loads from English suppliers.

Drawing from European designs, or the more basic and utility pioneering styles, American antique furniture is gaining a strong following. It should be of interest to the antique amateur, and the cheaper products are definitely something the amateur should consider.

English, American, Continental or Oriental — so many different types of antique furniture are on the market that it can be confusing. Just remember what I said at the beginning of this chapter: "Buy what you like and can afford from a reputable dealer and it is sure to appreciate over time."

One more thing before I go on to two other antique categories. As beginners first start looking at antique furniture, they will notice an abundance of English products on the market. There are three reasons for this.

First, English furniture design is one with which the majority of Americans are familiar, so it is the most popular.

The fact that England has a never-ending supply of affordable antique furniture is the second reason for its popularity. Of course people would much rather continue to buy things that will match what's already decorating their home, wouldn't they?

The third reason for the popularity of English antiques is because auctioneers are able to get large quantities fairly easily from English suppliers. Unlike Chinese antiques, English antique furniture is in ready supply as new housing replaces the old cottages in most English cities. Therefore, if priced right, it is the furniture of choice for most antique dealers who need only go to an nearby auction to restock. Since most auctions are open to the public, this is also the way an antique beginner should buy. My first book, *Money From Antiques,* provides auction buying techniques in great detail.

Having discussed the various origins of antique furniture, I will now discuss two other categories. These do not fall into a specific country or period of manufacture. They span such boundaries due to their basic styles. They are now called pine furniture or country, farm, or rural furniture.

Pine Furniture: Pine furniture gained popularity some ten years ago and has continued to become stronger and more desirable for more and more areas of the home. It was initially used in modern kitchens for styling, and is now finding its way into bedrooms, living rooms, bathrooms and patios. While there is some American antique pine available (mainly in the form of the perforated bread cupboards), the main supply is

Pine furniture has continued to become more desirable for every room of the house.

The popularity of country furniture is growing by leaps and bounds.

The key is age and the distressed condition of the piece — the more distressed the better.

from England and Ireland where antique pine lumber is readily available from old churches. The most sought after products are pine dressers, kitchen tables, chests and wardrobes. Irish pine furniture is very popular on the American East coast due to the large Irish immigrant population. California is also a growing market.

Pine furniture comes in painted, stripped, or finished form with the main demand being for stripped pine. Due to demand, furniture manufactured from old pine is the most prevalent, and reputable antique dealers should always advise you whether the piece is a genuine antique or whether it's a new piece manufactured from antique lumber.

Incidentally, antique pine can be identified by the large knots in the wood. Modern pine is so fast growing that the knots are very small. Antique pine also has a golden look while new pine is white in color.

While on the subject of antique pine, never put any oil on it. Just wipe it down with a damp cloth or use only clear wax paste to keep the wood in good condition.

Most antique furniture comes from outside the U.S.

Recommendation: For the antique beginner, pine furniture is a good way to go. Try to purchase old English or Irish pieces both for investment and enjoyment purposes. Old pine church pews are popular as seating oddities.

Country or Rural Furniture

The popularity of country or rural furniture is growing by leaps and bounds. It's a furniture line that the beginner should definitely take a look at. The key to country or rural is age and the distressed condition of the piece — the more distressed the better. Since country furniture is found in all sorts of way-out places, it is something that the antique beginner can immediately get involved with, and will be able to compete against the professional antique dealer. Not only that, it's fun. What could be more fun than taking a trip into the country and finding a piece of old discarded furniture in some musty barn? Especially if you buy it for next to nothing!

The fun in country antiques is the wide range of products that abound. Kitchen tables, old chairs, boxes, stools and butcher blocks are much sought after. Large cream buckets, spinning wheels and other oddities are all used as decorative pieces more and more. As our modern world becomes more sterile, country furniture will increase in popularity.

Halltree — designed to fit into a hallway.

Recommendation: Country or rural furniture is definitely for the amateur antiquer. Anything goes, so if you can buy it for almost nothing, go for it! In *Money from Antiques* I suggested the types of customers who buy such items. This could help you sell your products if you are in the antiques business for profit as well as for enjoyment.

Terminology

The very fact that most antique furniture comes from outside the U.S. brings with it a whole host of strange terminology. To the amateur this can be very confusing. While most of the general terms are well known, here are some that you may not know.

Commode: At first sound this brings visions of a toilet to mind but a commode can also be a low cabinet or bureau, or a cupboard containing a washbowl as well as a toilet cover.

Halltree: This is a particularly English piece of furniture originally designed to fit into a hallway. Replete with hooks for coats and containers for rubber boots, it was an essential piece of furniture for English homes. English weather being as it is, halltrees were required to have metal pans to catch the rain water dripping off coats or boots and many had lift-up seats to store cleaning materials in.

Folio Stand: This is a book or magazine stand that got its name from a large sheet of paper folded in two. This was often used to store music sheets alongside a piano.

Partner's Desk: Called such because of its original purpose as a lawyer's or boss's desk, at which both the owner and a subject could sit facing each other. It's also called a pedestal desk because of its two-support structure.

Davenport: In British antiques lingo this means a small writing bureau. For what reason it also means a large sofa convertible into a bed, I have no idea!

Coffer: Technically a strongbox, this term means a bedding or storage box in antique terms. They were originally used to store valuable objects.

Gateleg: This term is used to describe tables with folded legs that are extended to support drop-leaf side panels. Gatelegs are usually arranged in pairs.

Bonhew de Jour.

Refectory: A refectory is a long, narrow table. This word came from the Latin refectorium — to refresh, or a room where refreshments were served, usually in a monastery.

Lowboy: A low, table-like chest of drawers. Where "boy" came from no one seems to know.

Ormolu: Imitation gold decoration made from copper and tin or zinc alloy.

Breakfront: A high, wide cabinet with the center section projecting beyond the end sections.

Bonheur de Jour: It means "painter of the day," and is a small, delicate desk on which one could paint.

Burr: A hard knot of wood. The term is often used when describing the type of wood used. For example, burr walnut means walnut that's harder than normal because it comes from a burr where the grains are tightly knotted.

Some of those words are strange, aren't they? Can you imagine trying to sell a Bonheur de Jour? Most people wouldn't know what you were talking about.

While in no way complete (that would take a book in itself), I hope that some of these everyday words are of interest.

In closing this chapter, I would like to offer some advice to the amateur antiquer. Whether you are buying for yourself or for resale, always make sure the condition of the antique is excellent. Take your time inspecting it, particularly at the back and in the corners. It may not seem important when the salesperson brushes off that small section of missing decoration, but just try replacing it! Not only that, but you'll be kicking yourself when you find out it devalues the antique by as much as 50 percent.

Louis XVI furniture will be in demand.

To illustrate how important this is, let me tell you about my own purchasing trip to Wales. I was late for an auction, and was rushing around when I spied a terrific cupboard and bid on it even though I had given it only a cursory look.

After my bid topped all others, I took my time inspecting the cupboard. To my horror, I found that not only were the back supports full of wood worm, but most of the back was also missing.

I managed to get out of that one with some persuasive talking and I don't feel bad about it. Most auction pieces are sold on an "as is" basis, but I felt the cupboard was sufficiently damaged to the point that the auctioneer should have at least mentioned it.

I would also suggest that as an antique amateur you stick to the small accessory pieces at first. While these may seem more expensive in relation to the big wardrobe units, they are also more in demand. While on the subject of buying, don't forget what I said about auctions. By purchasing at auctions you can save yourself up to 50 percent of the retail price. If you are unsure of how to bid, buy my books *Money From Antiques* and *More Money From Antiques*, in which I cover auction and Internet buying in detail.

In closing this chapter I am going to stick my neck out and mention a trend that I think will be hot for many years to come.

Nineteenth century Louis XV and Louis XVI furniture will be in demand, as will country furniture and sets of chairs and ornate dining tables. Display cabinets will continue to be good sellers as will pedestal writing desks, particularly those from the Georgian period.

Here are my price recommendations.

$1,500 and under: 17th and 18th century English oak furniture is a good buy as are tea caddies, occasional tables, chests of drawers and Windsor or Regency armchairs.

$1,500 to $5,000: Late 19th century French decorative furniture and mahogany or rosewood dinning sets, Victorian extending dining tables, and good quality Georgian presses are your best bet.

$5,000 or more: You should buy the best mid and late 19th century English and French furniture by known makers such as Holland, Paul Sormani etc. Sets of Georgian chairs, Georgian bookcases, late Victorian painted satinwood furniture and good mahogany Victorian curio cases are also worth consideration.

You should buy the best mid and late 19th century English furniture.

Furniture covers 70 percent of the antiques business.

Antique furniture, like antique ceramics, is the most traded line of products by both dealers and private buyers. With the addition of glassware and silverware — which we will cover in the next two chapters, furniture covers 70 percent of the antiques business. Since too much knowledge can be as bad as too little for a beginner, I have not gone into too much detail. That you'll pick up as your experience grows. Initially, you should aim for lots of practical knowledge of your immediate area.

That's enough about furniture. Let's visit glasswares next, shall we?

Chapter Four

Glassware

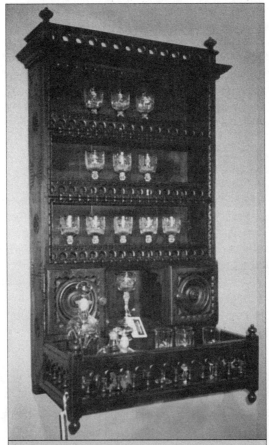

Antique glass is a product category dominated by a pool of very knowledgeable collectors.

As I began this chapter on glassware, and bearing in mind that this book is called *Antiques For Amateurs*, I was reminded of what an antique dealer friend of mine said to me when I first inquired about antique glass.

She told me antique glass is a product category full of inaccuracies and dominated by a huge pool of very knowledgeable amateur collectors.

That is still the case today. No other class of antiques has so many products with so much value resting on the opinions of so many. Antique glass is truly a free-for-all. It's also a Jekyll-and-Hyde-type category. While it is an important category with a large amount of products available, only a few products are well known enough to be anything more than a passing interest to the general public. Names or words like Depression glass, Carnival glass, Lalique and cobalt blue are known, but are just a minute segment of the overall antique glass picture. As a result, the bulk of antique glass is a very specialized part of the overall antique business. It is also a segment that fetches high prices for good, rare merchandise. Difficult to buy and sell, antique glass is an extremely specialized category and, with the space available, impossible to explain fully. For detailed information I recommend that you select your glass of preference and learn as much about it as you can by reading specialized literature and talking to dealers at glass shows, especially those held by glass collectors' associations.

Antique glass is classified first by period, then by country of origin or manufacturer. There are then only a few subcategories that fall into each of the groups. Glass is also occasionally classified by type. Thus there is English glass, Continental glass, and American glass, with Depression glass the mainstay of this latter section. Since Depression glass is of primary importance to American readers, I will begin with that. But first, here is a brief history of glassmaking which is a fascinating subject in itself. This thumbnail sketch doesn't do the material justice but it will give the amateur antiquer a brief overview of how glass migrated to the New Colonies.

The first glass was formed by lava from volcanoes in the Middle East and was known as volcanic obsidian. Used by early man, the obsidian was melted to form beads and bowls. Well before the metal age, glass was used in Egypt and Mesopotamia. Bottles have been found in the tomb of Thutmose I, who ruled Egypt from 1507 B.C. to 1497 B.C. Copied by the Greeks and then the Romans, glassmaking worked itself north to Venice, resulting in that town's rise in wealth. From there, the art of glassmaking spread through France, Germany and England. In 1608 glass became America's first industry, roughly a year after the first colonists arrived in Jamestown.

American Glass

Various types of antique glass were made in America during the 1850 to 1930 period. Broadly speaking, these types are:

Pressed Glass: This type is made by pressing melted glass into a mold with a weight. Carnival and Depression glass fall into this category.

Cut Glass: Made by cutting or engraving a design into the glass. Manufacturers include Heisey, Libbey and Son, Empire Cut Glass, Corona, Van heusen and Taylor Brothers.

Satin Glass: A dull, velvety-feeling, opaque glass with a white lining made by Mt. Washington Glass Co. of Bedford, Mass.

Colored Glass: Made from 1850 to the 1870s by pouring metal between two walls of clear blown glass to give a metallic look.

Of the above modes of manufacture, pressed Depression glass is by far the most popular.

Depression Glass: American antique glass is dominated by what is broadly called Depression glass with Carnival glass a close second. Both of these groupings consist of glassware primarily manufactured in the U.S., and as such they do not fit the strict definition of antiques since Depression glass was manufactured during the period 1920 to 1930. This is now being stretched to 1950 by most enthusiasts.

"Depression glass" is named so after the period of severe economic hardship that took place during the 1930s. Its pretty patterns and vast range of colors came to symbolize a better time through those dark, drab days. This could be the reason for its first growth in popularity during the early 60s and 70s, when economically, things improved. Isn't it strange how we always seem to remember the bad times more than the good? Just look how the two World Wars are so often remembered by ex-soldiers.

During the Great Depression period in American history, vast amounts of inexpensive, colored glassware were produced by a myriad of small French, German and English immigrant families who had migrated to areas such as Pennsylvania and Ohio, where electricity, rail transport, and the necessary sand was readily available. Most of it was translucent with clear, green, ruby red, pink, blue and avocado colors predominating. Although inexpensive then, Depression glass has one outstanding characteristic: Almost all pieces are of attractive, unusual and often complicated designs. They certainly do not look as if they were produced during a period of extreme hardship. Nor was the quality poor. It was as if the spirit of America was shining through and many Depression glass pieces are of the highest quality imaginable.

Manufacturers of Depression glass were many and varied. Jeanette Glass Co., Liberty Glass Works, McBeth Evans Glass Co., Indiana Glass Co., Anchor Hocking Glass Co., Imperial Glass Co. and Hazel Atlas Co. are just a few.

Where Depression glass gets confusing for the amateur is in the alphabetical designations and descriptive names given to specific pieces. For example: If something is an A pattern, the cup and saucer must be two different colors. The pattern pieces that came in a box of "Mothers Oats" were designated B patterns and the patterns most reproduced were the J and N patterns. Over and above this, specific designs were given descriptive women's names such as Aunt Polly, Katy Blue, Sharon "Cabbage Rose," and Lorain Basket. There are also patterns named for fruit, such as Cherryberry and Avocado, and patterns named after flowers such as Dogwood, Cloverleaf, and Iris. As you can see, you need to be an expert to understand Depression glass. As if this isn't enough, men's names such as Patrick, Adam, and Vernon are also used to indicate specific types.

Based on what I've said above, you probably know what my advice is for the amateur antiquer interested in glass. Forget it? No, not at all. Depression glass is too important for that.

An antique amateur should spend time studying Depression glass by reading literature from Krause Publications, Kovel, Crown Publishers and a million others before you venture out to buy and sell Depression glass. I have given you a brief overview, but this subject requires you read numerous books to gain adequate information. The more you can absorb by reading specialized literature and visiting Depression glass shows, the more experienced you will become. Words like Fire King and Ruby Red, and strange dinnerware descriptions like Philbe and Jane Ray will then become part of your vocabulary.

Recommendation: For amateurs interested in collecting, I highly recommend Depression glass. Large quantities were made and it can be found in grandmas' attics from coast to coast. Flea markets, garage sales and thrift stores are also full of it. For someone interested in antiques as a commercial proposition I would advise you avoid Depression glass. Purchases mainly come from enthusiasts wanting the most competitive prices and it's hard to maintain normal retail markups with Depression glass. There are just too many amateurs collecting it to make it a viable commercial business.

Carnival Glass: Carnival glass is iridescent, colored glass manufactured between 1900 and 1920 in large quantities. It was a cheap glass with lots of repeat copies. The main manufacturers were Northwood (N) Glass Co. of Martin's Ferry, Ohio, Imperial Glass (IG) of Dellaire, Ohio, and Fenton Glass Co. of Williamstown, W.Va. Other well known manufacturers were Westmoreland Glass Co., Dagenhart Glass and St. Clair Glass. To give the antiquer a sense of the volume of Carnival glass made, here are four brief histories.

St. Clair: Founded in 1885 by John St. Clair, an immigrant from Alsace-Lorraine, France, the St. Clair glassworks passed through his son's hands, his grandsons John, Paul, Joseph, Edward and Robert and finally ended with Joe's death in 1987. The St. Clair family was known for unusual handmade pieces and collector's items. Glass trains, reclining horses, and paneled cream and sugar jugs were their specialty.

Westmoreland Glass Co.: Incorporated in 1888 in Grapeville, near Jeannette, Penn., Westmoreland manufactured candy and mustard jars by the thousands. Famous for their White Milk glass, Westmoreland also manufactured items from L.G. Wright's molds, their distributor. It is these limited edition items that are prized by collectors. Levay, another distributor, had the same arrangement and used special colors. The Buzz Star Punch set in Black Carnival is very rare — only thirty-one sets were made.

Fenton Art Glass Co.: Founded in Martins Ferry, Ohio, in 1905 by Frank L. Fenton and his brothers John W. and Charles H., Fenton glass is known for its beauty. One of the most important glass factories still in existence today, its early Carnival golden iridescence, opalescence in blue, yellow and green, and its ruby crystal, are sought after by collectors worldwide. Items produced in abundance during the 1908 to 1921 years are famous and fetch high prices on the antique market.

Degenhart Glass: Famous for its glass paperweights, Degenhart Glass was founded in 1901 by Arthur J. Bennet who hired John Degenhart for his German glassblowing skills. In 1947, after years of scrimping and saving, John and Elizabeth Degenhart founded the Crystal Art Glass factory, and began to manufacture their famous overlay cobalt window paperweight, which featured George and Martha Washington with an olive branch. The paperweight consisted of a cube of white glass embedded in clear crystal with an overlay of cobalt blue, and only three were made. One is in the Burgstrum Paperweight Museum, one is privately owned and Mrs. Degenhart has the third. John Degenhart's paperweights with roses in blue, yellow, and red, with black diamond dust are world famous.

Carnival glass items were manufactured in many forms and form a very important segment of American glassmaking history.

Tiffany Glass

"Color is to the eye as music is to the ear." —Louis Comfort Tiffany (1848-1933).

Who hasn't heard of Tiffany glass? Associated with leaded glass lamps, Louis Comfort Tiffany's glassware fetches astronomical prices at London and New York auctions. Born in New York, this painter and designer of Art Nouveau decorative-glass objects studied under American artists George Inness and Samuel Colman before going to Paris.

When he returned to New York, he established his glassmaking factory and is best known for his opalescent glass, known as Tiffany Favrile glass, which is used in decorative windows, lamps and other objects d'art.

Many reproduction Tiffany lamps exist, but occasionally an original surfaces. Tiffany's original Dragonfly and Lotus lamps are the standard by which other antique lamp manufacturers are measured. Though renowned for lamps, Tiffany's stained glass stands as an example of the diversity of the material.

Tiffany also manufactured other products including vases. Originals are valuable and sell quickly to enthusiastic collectors. They're easily identified and always carry the Tiffany markings.

To conclude this section on American antique glass, I want to mention that I have barely scratched the surface with this brief overview. Very strong in the U.S., Depression glass and Carnival glass form the bulk of the antique glass business. Tiffany stands out as a shining light.

English Glassware

English glassware, like furniture, is classified by periods. Victorian (1837-1901), Georgian (1714-1830) and Edwardian (1901-1910) are all popular reigns. English glassware covers cut glass, crystal, and miscellaneous colored glass. It also encompasses a larger range of products than American antique glass. Often combined with wood or silver, English antique glass includes decanter sets, cruet sets and chandeliers. Vases, scent bottles, drinking glasses of various stem lengths and cream jugs are but a part of these popular antique collectibles.

For the antique beginner, English glass offers a wide variety of products. Because prices in the U.S. are considerably lower than those in England, finding a market for such items is difficult. A number of English glassware product lines stand out.

Decanters: Plain, engraved, heavy cut, or crystal, 17th and 18th century decanters are widely traded. Often sold in pairs or sets of three, strong demand keeps European prices in the four-figure bracket. Silver mounted decanters are readily available and late Victorian era Claret pieces are still found at reasonable prices. When purchasing decanters, an antiquer should ensure that the stoppers are original, undamaged, and that the rim and decanter as a whole are unchipped. As I stated before: Condition in antiques is everything and decanter stoppers are often lost or broken. Without its original stopper, the value of a decanter plummets.

Drinking glasses: Rummers, tumblers, ale glasses, wine glasses, claret glasses and goblets; English drinking glasses come in all sizes and in all varieties. Georgian "lead glass," invented by George Ravenscroft in the late 17th century, is a find. Stem shapes are important — the fancier the better. Trumpet bowl designs fetch good prices. Once again, condition is essential.

For the beginner, English glass offers a wide variety of products.

Jugs: Soda, cream, water, and claret jugs are in the lower priced range of English glass. Style is very important here — the fancier, the better.

Scent bottles: A collector's favorite, scent bottles are in tremendous demand. Their popularity has grown in recent years, with prices topping $5,000 for rare, difficult-to-find perfume bottles. As an antique beginner you can't go wrong buying any you come across. The price is sure to continue escalating.

When discussing glassware one must not forget Irish glass, Bristol Blue cobalt, and glass candlesticks.

Irish glass: 17th and 18th century Irish glass is considered in high esteem by antique buffs. Salt and pepper containers, decanters, preserve dishes and butter dishes are excellent buys and value increases considerably with a good provenance. For the beginner, Irish glass is interesting because so many unusual items can be found. Pickle jars, toddy lifters, unusual wine urns and even boat-shaped fruit bowls add interest to Irish glass collecting.

Here's a side note worth remembering: If you have the time, research the piece of glass you're selling. Look in an atlas, and find the interesting features of the town in which your flagons, rummers, etc., originated. The best work was produced between 1760 and 1830. Original supplies of cobalt blue came from Saxony and were cut off by the Napoleonic Wars, after which Bristol became the center of cobalt blue production.

Mirrors: While not necessarily glass products, mirrors could be considered part of the family. Manufactured throughout the Georgian, Victorian and Regency period, English mirrors are in high demand due to their extremely ornate gilt, mahogany, satinwood and metal frames. The same can be said of various gilt mirrors made in France during the King Louis periods.

While not necessarily glass products, mirrors could be considered part of the family.

Lovely to look at, and often depicting a story, antique stained glass is gaining popularity by leaps and bounds.

Mirrors are an excellent antique line for the beginner. Not only are they pleasing products to the eye, they are also useful decorative items for the home. In addition they fetch high prices. Who doesn't want an antique mirror in the hallway, even if your house is full of modern furniture? Highly recommended for the antique amateur, mirrors are the glass and furniture "sleeper."

Stained glass windows: No antique guidebook would be complete without mentioning stained glass windows. They're lovely to look at and often depict a story (often Christian). Antique stained glass is gaining popularity in leaps and bounds. Prices are also rising due to limited supply and stained glass windows such as "Minstrel with Cymbals" by William Morris and "Mary" by Edward Burne-Jomes sell for $20,000 and up. Having said that, many English stained glass church windows are available on the market at reasonable prices and these are what the amateur should look for. They are sure to appreciate in value rapidly if the glass is in excellent condition. Just remember, leave the frames as they are. The weathered look is what decorators are looking for. As a guide, watch for the intricate, detailed pieces.

Continental glass consists of French, German, Bohemian, and Italian products.

Crystal is a high quality glass, both leaded and unleaded.

Continental Glass

Continental glass consists of French, German, Bohemian, and Italian products. Among the myriad of manufacturers, Frenchmen Rene Lalique and Emille Gallé stand out.

Lalique: Rene Lalique was a Parisian goldsmith, but in 1908, when he was 50, a perfume producer asked him to design a glass label for an existing flagon. Glass fascinated him and with his extraordinary artistic skills he created vases, tableware, lamps and perfume bottles. Fixated by the perfume bottle's symbolism of luxury and beauty he created more than 250 unique perfume bottles between 1908 and 1937. Today, these are extremely rare collector's items. In 1928, a set of Lalique glasses was used at the Elysee Palace. An avant-garde with his frosted swirl designs, antique collectors love Lalique's unusual creations, many that incorporate beautiful naked female figures. Medium to extremely high priced, Lalique glass is a high-end product line.

Emille Gallé: Born in 1846, Emille Gallé began producing exquisitely colored glassware in Nancy, France. Starting with clear and enameled glass, he progressed to stratified, acid-etched, and wheel-carved glass with a Japanese design. In 1889 his work was exhibited at the Paris Exposition. This helped him establish his Japanese cameo vases, which are distinguished by their bright colors and attention to detail.

Daum Glassworks, Nancy: Ranked up there with Lalique and Galle, Auguste and Antonin Daum started manufacturing their thick-walled, deeply etched, geometric cameo designs in the early 1870s. They manufactured plate glass and tableware under the name Verriere St. Catherine, and in 1890 they changed to floral cameo items. Daum's deeply etched floral vases are their trademark, along with their use of noted artists such as Salvador Dali. Such antiques fetch five and six figures when sold at auction.

Bohemian glass: Bohemia, now part of the Czech Republic, has a history of glassmaking dating back to the 14th century. It's known for its crystal and engraved perfume bottles, glass jewelry, and more recently Art Nouveau engraving by manufacturers such as Loetz. Bohemian glass is the Cinderella of antique glass collecting. Production of the famous Bohemian glass was interrupted by the World Wars and Communist rule. Now coming back into its own, Bohemian glass items such as 1855 drinking glasses by artists such as Wenzel Reif are developing a small, but increasingly enthusiastic following.

Venetian glass: Venetian glassmaking stretches back to the 15th and 16th century when Cristallo (perfectly clear) glass was able to corner the market. Items such as round, funnel-bowl ale glasses are occasionally still found. But, as a general rule, Venetian glass holds little interest for the American antiquer because of its scarcity on the American market.

Antique crystal: Crystal is a high quality glass, both leaded and unleaded. Antique crystal is generally classified in the glass category and products from Swarovski, Stuart, Webb and Corbett, and Waterford can be found in most antique sales. Some Bohemian crystal is available in Europe but such products are very scarce in the United States.

We have come to the end of another chapter, and again we've covered a lot of ground. While it has not made you an expert, this chapter has given you an intelligent overview of antique glassware that will enable you to hold your own with most enthusiasts and dealers. Before summarizing, here are some commonly used glass words and their meanings. I like adding these because they are both fun and educational.

Baluster: Used in reference to a drinking glass' stem, it means a post or support.

Knop: Often used with other descriptions such as "air beaded," knop means a decorative knob.

Tantalus: A stand for displaying decanters, often of the lockup type.

Rummer: A large drinking cup or glass, originally used for rum.

Firing Glass: A short dram or wine glass with an especially strong, thick foot. Used at meetings, firing glasses would be struck on the table to indicate enthusiasm after a member's toast. When this was done the thick glass made a sound resembling the firing of a musket.

Imagine.

Imagine: A large vaulted hall, stained glass windows, long wooden refectory tables and benches, men in top coats with top hats and gloves on the tables, walking canes in their hands, all raising rummers to the speaker and then drumming the glasses on the tables. Fun, isn't it? All that is needed to make this picture complete is a couple of little urchin boys peeking in through the crack in a side door.

Toddy: A brandy or other liquor mixed with hot water, sugar and spices. A toddy lifter was therefore a toddy glass or decanter.

Gadrooned: A band of convex, ornamental molding with reeding or beading design.

These are just a few of the strange words used in the antique glass business. Most general dealers keep a book on descriptions handy in case an expert tries to baffle them. If you're dealing in antique glassware extensively, this would be a good idea.

Recommendation. The amateur antiquer should stick to Depression and Carnival glass because of its large following, vast amount of available product, and steadily increasing prices. If you do, you will find a huge following to network with.

Five-thousand dollars and above: cut glass clusters.

Here are my suggestions.

$1,500 and under — Any Depression or Carnival glass, 18th century drinking glasses, candlesticks and clear glass plates.

$1,500 to $5,000 — Bristol Blue cream jugs, engraved wine glasses and pickle jars.

$5,000 or more — Ormula and cut glass clusters and silver and crystal decanters.

Summary

The antique beginner will find glassware both a fascinating and complex subject.

Depending on whether you are interested in collecting for yourself or as an investment, your approach will be different.

As an enthusiast, antique glass is worth collecting. It will give you many hours of pleasure as well as a little bit of profit.

As a budding antiques dealer, I would suggest that you avoid glassware. It is little known in the general antique retail business and sales are limited to enthusiastic collectors who know prices by heart and are always looking for a bargain. Far better to invest in ceramics or better still, antique furniture. Silverware, which we shall cover next, is also a better product line if you intend to enter the antiques business purely for profit.

Chapter Five

Silver

Antique silver product lines are extensive and as such, they offer many opportunities.

Antique silver is both decorative and practical. For these reasons it is a popular antique product line with a large, general demand. As with most antiques, the bigger the market, the easier it is to buy and sell. Therefore, antique silver is a promising area for the amateur.

Like many antique products, silver can be split into English, Continental, and American, with English and American predominating. A further division can be made into genuine hallmarked silver and silver plate. Both materials are worth the amateur's attention.

Real antique silver is a valuable commodity and antique silver products are relatively pricey. Because the value of silverware is tied to the spot price of silver on the London precious metal market on any given day, prices of silverware fluctuate considerably.

Antique silver product lines are extensive and they afford the amateur an opportunity at some smaller and cheaper pieces, then allow them to move up the ladder to items that sell in the upper five-figure bracket. With this in mind I shall discuss English and American silver history before covering specific product lines.

English Silver

English silver products, like furniture, are classified by Royalty periods first and by manufacturer's name second. The same Georgian, Victorian and Regency periods that are used to date antique furniture are also used when dating English silver. Design detail also follows the same decorative or plain patterns. Early Georgian is therefore plainer, while Victorian silver is most times highly decorative.

Victorian baskets are one of antique silver's mainstays.

The manufacture of silver items in England spans a vast period, stretching from the early 14th century through to its peak during the Georgian-Edwardian period (1714-1910). It is this latter period of English, Scottish and Irish manufacture of products that most concerns the present day antique dealer. Names like Taylor and Perry, Paul Storr, Robert Gerrard, James Dixon and Sons, Walker and Hall and George Edwards all feature products ranging from delicate sugar baskets to large, elaborate candelabras. More important than the manufacturer, however, is the period of manufacture, hallmark identification, and type of item. These three factors govern prices with London, Birmingham or Glasgow as the most desired places of manufacture.

As mentioned, hallmarks detail a piece's genuine silver composition, its authenticity and its history. An amateur should purchase a book detailing all the hallmark signs before purchasing sterling silver. Having it handy when out on a buying expedition will prove invaluable.

With that in mind let us cover some silver items, periods, and design characteristics.

Baskets: Popular and highly decorative, George IV, V and Victorian silver fruit, bread, cake and sweetmeat baskets are an antique silver mainstay. Victorian period shell-shaped or dolphin foot baskets by manufacturers such as William Gibson or George Fox are highly prized with top pieces fetching $10,000 and up. Smaller sugar or cake baskets with swing handles are always in demand at $500 plus. If found, sets of baskets reach exceptional prices at auctions and the 1800 to very early 1900 period is what an antique amateur should look for.

Advice: Highly decorative engraved pieces are what you should use as a guide, but any Georgian or Victorian basket you can buy is a good bet.

Beakers and Bowls: George II, III, and Victorian bowls and beakers are great finds. The 1700 period pieces, particularly Irish ones, are in demand but the same basic guide — high decoration, complete sets, and good provenance — drive beaker and bowl prices up.

Advice: This segment of the antique sterling silver market is restricted by supply. Better to concentrate on items with wider availability.

Silver Boxes: What a variety! And so interesting. Jewel caskets and card cases, plus trinket, pill, tobacco, and knickknack boxes fill this category. In addition, there's also larger toilet boxes and even biscuit barrels that make some bigger pieces part of the top end of this product line. These are the antique amateur's dream. This category is where you can let your imagination go wild since the only guide to a good buy is the hallmark and period of manufacture.

Advice: Boxes are an excellent antique silver product line for the amateur. The variety available means that boxes are both a collectible and a general interest item.

Candelabras and Candlesticks: The heavyweight class of antique silver, this is where demand and high prices meet. George II to George V and Victorian items are forever in demand, with decorated candelabras taking second place to pairs or sets of candlesticks. You noticed I said pairs or sets. That is important. Single candlesticks do not reach anywhere near the good pro rata price pairs do because candlesticks are still used in the home and single ones are not as decorative as a matched pair. More than in any other silver line, the name of the artist is important. Robert Gerrard 1820 pieces, sets by John Cafe and pairs of chamber sticks (short stems with a carrying hook) designed by Paul Storr in London in the 1820s are items you should seek. Candlesticks with crests, such as those of the Earl of Cork (1767-1856), fetch terrific prices and these are still occasionally available. If you find any with a design that even resembles a crest, coronet, or coat of arms, buy them. Other artists to remember are Samuel Whitford of London, John Lloyd of Dublin and Henry Wilkinson & Co. of Sheffield.

Candlesticks and candelabras are a very desirable segment of the antique business and I would recommend that an amateur get involved in collecting or trading in silver candlesticks. Prices range from $500 for a simple chamber stick to more than $20,000 for sets of top Georgian sticks, so there is room for everybody.

Casters: Highly collectible silver casters (salt and pepper shakers) by Walker and Hall of London are the benchmark of these items. Victorian and Georgian pieces again dominate. As an amateur you should buy shakers in pairs and make sure that their condition is good. Heavy corrosion from salt detracts from value.

Advice: Casters are a good collectible at reasonable prices for the antique beginner.

Trophies: The Cinderella of silver, antique cups maintain limited demand. Scottish and famous trophy cups fetch low four-figure sales figures, but their manufacture to commemorate specific events restricts interest from anyone but sports enthusiasts.

Advice: Silver trophies are not recommended for the beginner due to their limited demand.

Coffee and Chocolate Pots: These pots are separated from teapots mainly because of their shape, height and combinations of accessories. Coffee and chocolate pots are bigger, (10 to 12 inches), taller (almost twice the height of teapots) and often fitted with wooden handles. Ornate George III and George IV coffeepots are much sought after but matched pairs of cafe au lait pots are sold at reasonable prices. The antique beginner interested in Coffee and Chocolate pots should look for items with flower and foliage scrolls as well as curved handles.

Advice: This is a good item for the antique beginner.

Silver trophies have a limited demand.

George III and George IV coffee pots are much sought after.

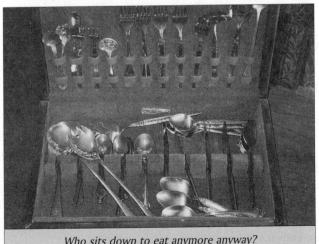

Who sits down to eat anymore anyway?

Victorian inkstands are still reasonably priced.

Cutlery: Silver antique cutlery in complete settings is difficult to come by. Partial settings, on the other hand, are plentiful. Old English Victorian cutlery such as the King pattern is in demand, especially the monogrammed elaborate sets that come in beautiful wooden cabinets. For the antique amateur, cutlery sets are not recommended. They cost more than $5,000 and have a limited market since modern homes have fewer family members and smaller dining rooms. Who sits down to eat anymore, anyway?

Sterling silver spoons fall into another category, however, as many spoons are of the commemorative variety. Since it is a very important silver category, I will cover commemorative spoons in Chapter Seven.

Inkstands: A terrific silver line. English silver inkstands come in many designs and the beginner needs to make sure all the pieces that make up a set are included. Older 16th century pieces fetch high prices but Victorian inkstands are still reasonably priced when found.

Used as decorative items in studies, lawyer's and accountant's offices and business premises, silver inkstands are excellent items for the beginner to buy.

Mugs and tankards: This is another great silver product for the antique beginner. Seventeenth century tankards inscribed by Samuel Welles, Charles Fox and Humphrey Payne London are quite popular, particularly the ones with elaborate handles. Many mugs have plain bodies but if their condition is good, they are in demand. My suggestion for the beginner is to collect items from the same period.

Salvers: Currently very popular, silver salvers can be found at any auction or antique mall. They're reasonably priced, and many households have one on the sideboard that is often used as a fruit bowl. Georgian salvers are the most popular, followed by Victorian. A good product for the beginner, silver salvers with elaborate borders are the ones you should concentrate on.

Edwardian tea sets are also popular.

Tea Sets: English tea sets are by far the most popular silver product. Used as much for decoration as for serving tea, silver tea sets are perfect antique products for the beginner. When dealing in English silver, Victorian sets are the ticket. Three and four-piece sets with rocaille scroll molded spouts, tendril handles and gilt interiors made in London during the 1800s are the sets most desired. Ensure that the pieces are all part of the same set and are fully hallmarked for maximum value.

Sets by H.W. Curry of London, John Sherwood and Sons of Birmingham, and McKay and Chisholm of Edinburgh are much desired. If you can find matching sugar tongs it increases the set's value by 20 percent. Sets with the additional coffee pots should be your first choice when you buy; however, highly detailed three-piece sets are also desirable. If you find them with a matching tray, don't hesitate to buy a complete silver tea set.

Edwardian tea sets, while not as elaborate as the Victorian ones, are also popular. These are often found with wooden handles and if you can find them in the $1,000 range, they are a good buy. I have even seen a 1925 Paul Storr six-piece replica set, made in Sheffield, that consisted of merely a spirit kettle, teapot, hot water jug, sugar bowl, milk jug, slop basin, two stands and an oval serving tray that sold for $12,000.

Advice: English silver tea sets are an excellent product line, especially those in first class condition. As a decorative item they are in constant demand. This ensures that prices will continue to increase steadily.

Single Teapots: As part of the tea set line, single teapots are also in demand. Because they are single items, their prices are reasonable and again, I highly recommend silver teapots as they are very suitable to the beginner. English Georgian teapots are the ones you should try to find. If fitted with wooden handles, all the better. Once again, condition is important. The Tannin in tea leaves is corrosive and if the spout is badly corroded it devalues the pot by 50 percent so check the product thoroughly. If you can find an English teapot engraved with a coat of arms be sure to buy it. It will fetch a good price either in England or in the U.S.

Which brings me to the oft-asked question: "How can I sell an antique piece in England where it will fetch a higher price than in the States?"

My advice is as follows: Go to the bookstore and look up reputable auctioneers or dealers in England advertising in the Miller Price Guide. Contact them via mail, phone or the Internet. You will find that many of them are highly experienced in selling items on behalf of American clients. Use insured UPS or FedEx parcel service to guarantee safe transportation to the UK. If you're hesitant about selling, request the auctioneer to put a reserve price on the items for sale. Most will do this if the product is valued at over five-hundred pounds ($800 plus). Just be reasonable. There's no point in setting the price so high that there's no chance of selling the goods. Also, ask the auctioneer to pay you with a dollar money order or bank-to-bank transfer. Expect this to cost you a 10 percent service charge.

Before closing out English silver, here is another suggestion about purchasing items in England.

Many reputable, well-established English auction houses are now on the Internet. You can put in an absent bid using your credit card on items advertised. This opens up your purchasing market considerably. For those interested in more details I suggest my book *More Money From Antiques,* in which I cover Internet buying comprehensively.

Having digressed slightly, let us complete the product lines, shall we?

Tea Caddies: Silver tea caddies, like the wooden ones, are the peak of this product line. Difficult to find but much in demand, silver tea caddies fetch high prices on the antique market. Georgian ones are the period of choice but if you're lucky enough to come across any, I would suggest that you snap it up. It is sure to appreciate in value dramatically.

Silver Tureens: Antique silver tureens are quite large and are expensive products for the beginner. The weight of silver alone ensures this. Georgian period tureens are the most popular ones with highly decorated Victorian ones a close second. My advice to a beginner is to avoid tureens initially. You would be better off investing the money in teapots where demand ensures a reasonable price and a constant demand.

Miscellaneous: Dressing mirrors, children's rattles, pepperettes, sugar and cake nips (tongs), presentation trowels, figurines, decanter label, etc. The list of miscellaneous silver antiques is endless. I once even bought

The list of miscellaneous silver antiques is endless.

Sheffield plate is a layer of genuine silver over copper beaten together to give the silver a warm glow.

a Victorian lemon squeezer, which gave me endless hours of amusement when no one could identify what it was. All highly desirable, English antique silver products are a must for the antique beginner.

The English antique silver terminology is a long section and will give the amateur an overview of the considerable amount of product out there. English silver antiques are highly recommended, as they have become quite scarce in the marketplace. I have even heard of an English dealer buying up silver pieces in America to supplement his English stock.

English Silver Plate: Not much recognized for many years, English silver plate is gaining popularity due to the number of unusual items suddenly becoming collectors' pieces. Decanter labels on silver chain are an obvious example, but old Sheffield plate three-light candleholders, bacon dishes with revolving lids, Sheffield plate kettle-on-a-stand and Georgian wine coasters are also suddenly desired by the antique trade. Silver plate corkscrews leapt to the top of the collector's list with the growing popularity of wine products as did mid-Victorian wine ewers and matching goblets. Silver plate wine coolers are extremely popular with the William IV period having produced many beautiful, ornate examples. That's the fascinating thing about the antiques business; one never knows which direction it will shoot off in next. Who would have thought that the surge in the popularity of wine would bring to light so many interesting silver plate collectibles?

One thing I should mention. Being the sharp-eyed beginner you are, you may have noticed that I mentioned Sheffield plate a number of times. Sheffield plate is a layer of genuine silver over copper, which is beaten together to give the silver a warm glow. That's important. The value of silver antiques depends very much on whether it is solid silver, Sheffield plate, or silver plate. Good plate means the product will stay in mint condition.

That also means you shouldn't clean it with anything but soap and slightly warm water. Wiping with a soft cloth finishes the job. The minute the silver starts to flake the antique's value drops drastically. My recommendation is to stick with Sheffield plate or a well known London plater such as J.W. Story and William Elliot of London.

That brings English silver to a close. I have gone to such lengths over the various product lines because 70 percent of the antique silver in America is of English origin. Now let's look at American silver, shall we?

Spoons, forks, and tongs.

American Silver

There isn't the vast array of American silver products as there are English ones. Some handmade items were produced by William Gorham, Dominick, and Tiffany, but American antique silver consists mainly of flatware and hollowware. Some 1904 Art Nouveau pieces by Durgin and products such as 1912 sugar bowls and creamers by companies like Revere Silver Co. of New York do, however, find a ready market. Products from late 1800s artists like Whiting and Colonial Massachusetts Silversmiths also have a following.

American silver, while far more scarce than English, nevertheless offers an antiques beginner opportunities. Look for examples such as an 1898 fruit bowl by Jacobi and Jenkins, Baltimore, Md. Decorated with a frieze of acanthus leaves, various flowers and foliage this 8-inch-high bowl would be worth approximately $1,500. Jacobi and Jenkins jam spoons are also good buys. Such items offer the beginner a good opportunity for profit, as do candlesticks, napkin rings and medallions by Towles, nut and sugar bowls by Gorham, and gray ladles, spoons, forks and tongs by Frank Whiting.

While on the subject of American silver I must mention the silver dollar. I will not get into precious coins as it is such a specialized subject that an amateur shouldn't get involved without expert advice. This story might however give you an idea how high priced some antiques are.

The 1804 American silver dollar, of which there are only fifteen examples known, has set records for rare coins. One of the reasons is that mystery surrounds the 1804 coin due to it not being struck by the U.S. Mint in Philadelphia. Where it was struck is still occupying the minds of the best coin collectors throughout the world.

In 1989 a silver dollar known as the "Dexter Dollar" sold for $990,000, but this was quickly eclipsed in April, 1997, when $1,815,000 was paid for the "Stickney" specimen of the same coin. Wow! Just imagine if you ever found one of those!

Having digressed with that interesting story, let's take a brief look at Continental silver.

Silver chatelaines are very collectible.

Continental Silver

Eighteenth century Irish, Dutch, French and Russian silver pieces are the benchmark in continental silver, with Spanish and Turkish silver items following hard on their heels. Very few of these pieces reach America, let alone emerge on the general market. When they do, they tend to be snuff boxes, beakers, and candlesticks. Markings on continental silver are also harder to decipher and I would recommend that before buying you do some research through the library or Internet. One type of continental silver product that is found on the East Coast is Dutch and German caskets.

If you are particularly interested in continental silver and live near concentrations of immigrants, I would suggest that you visit small local ethnic antique stores where items brought over by their compatriots are on sale. Bear in mind that resale value is governed by demand and that such items will not be of interest to the general antique business. For this reason, I do not recommend beginners become involved in such items. One continental silver item that bucks this trend is Vesta cases. These religious items interest a wider range of customers and as such they have a greater market.

As you can see by the length of the various sections on silver, English silver items dominate the general antique business. Although supply is drying up, they are a category of antiques that a beginner should get involved in. Here are some of the more obscure terms used in the silver antique business.

Rococo Cartouche: Fanciful asymmetrical 17th century French artistic design on scroll-like space used for an inscription or to serve as an ornament.

Cabochon: Highly polished convex shape used to describe short leg supports on silver bowls or bread baskets.

Gadroon: A band of convex, ornamental reeding or beading often found on Victorian silver baskets.

Acanthus scrolls: A large segmented, thistle-like acanthus leaf design often found on Corinthian columns and on 17th century silver.

Epergne: A center piece frame with extended arms often found on Victorian desert stands.

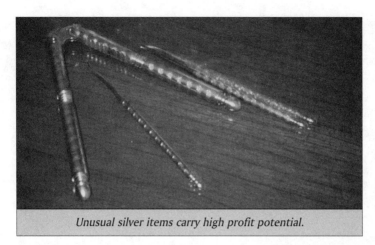

Unusual silver items carry high profit potential.

Arabesques: An Arabian ornate design made up of intertwined floral and foliate designs often found on antique coffee pots.

Salt/Casters: Antique salt, mustard, and pepper containers.

Pepperette: As it sounds — a silver pepper shaker, often plated.

Necessaire: A container, usually containing pins, needles, thread and sewing tools.

Argyle: Usually indicates a Scottish tartan but when used to describe silver it means a cylindrical tea pot.

Ribbon Threader: A most unusual silver item. With the back end looking like a scissors handle with finger holes and the front often designed in the form of a bird with opening beak, ribbon threaders are fascinating items. If the beak comes with a hole in it the item was used for threading thread, if without, it was used as a sugar nip. If you ever see such a ribbon threader, buy it — it's a most unusual silver item. Now you will probably be the only person who knows what it is.

Chatelaine: A silver or gilt belt holder containing sewing items such as a pin cushion, thimble and scissors. Very collectible, particularly the full silver ones.

Aren't those descriptions interesting? Also confusing! That's the fun in antiques. The terminology includes so many old fashioned words that just learning a few enables you to flaunt your knowledge.

As this chapter comes to a close, here are my recommendations for the antique beginner interested in silver antiques.

Recommendation: Following the premise that the larger the segment of the market, the easier it is for the beginner to enter I would suggest that you definitely consider silver antiques. My recommendation is that you mix English teapots and candlesticks with unusual items. That way you will have two very tradable lines with high profit potential. The teapots and candlesticks should be Georgian or Victorian and as ornate as possible. Always ensure that they are hallmarked, and if possible have artist's or maker's names inscribed.

Silver inkstands are another terrific specialty.

Unusual silver items will give you a line of products that carry high profit potential. corkscrews, ribbon threaders, chatelaines, Victorian lemon squeezers, decanter labels and unusual sugar nips all generate interest and subsequently, profit. Silver inkstands are another terrific specialty — lawyers and accountants use them for decorative items in their offices and you know how much money they make!

From a price point of view, here are my recommendations:

> $1,500 and under — I would suggest that unusual items are your best bet. Vesta cases, pepperettes, even small silver framed dressing table mirrors are items to go for.

> $1,500 to $5,000 — I recommend sets of tea and coffee pots and pairs or sets of candlesticks.

> $5,000 or more — top quality snuff boxes, and large items like punch bowl sets are your best buy.

Summary

Silver products like ceramics and furniture are a must for the serious antique amateur. If you are a collector it is a product line that will give you many hours of satisfaction as well as considerable profit. Condition in silver products is everything. Damaged items do not appreciate anywhere near as fast as mint condition ones.

With the end of this chapter we have covered the four main antique product lines — ceramics, furniture, glass and silver. Now we are going to discuss interesting second tier products starting with jewelry. Stay with me. It should be fun.

Chapter Six

Jewelry

Antique jewelry falls into the categories of precious, semi-precious, and costume jewelry.

M ost ladies' eyes light up as soon as they approach the first antique jewelry booth in a mall. Men, on the other hand, gaze nostalgically at the military collectibles. Who said men and women are equal?

Well, they may be equal, but their tastes are quite different.

As many women enter the antique business, they often gravitate to jewelry as their main line of business. Therefore it's not surprising that this is one of the fastest growing segments in the antique business. But such fast growth may prove to be a problem. Demand is outpacing supply — and as a result prices are rising. For women interested in antique jewelry this results in both positive and negative challenges. To take advantage of the opportunities you need to know the basics.

Antique jewelry falls into precious, semi-precious and costume jewelry segments. Within these there are Art Deco and Art Nouveau sections. Surprisingly, the line between precious, semi-precious and costume jewelry is often blurred. Without specialized knowledge this trend can be dangerous, as large sums of money are often lost in the first rush of enthusiasm. An amateur antiquer, therefore, must learn as much about precious stones as possible before venturing into jewelry. As the lines between precious and non-precious jewelry blur, you could lose a lot of money if you aren't on your toes.

First, let's consider the basics. Since my aim is to give a beginner an overall assessment as well as useful advice, I looked for the parameters that govern both

Victorian jewelry case.

supply and demand only to find that there are so many variables in antique jewelry that it is probably the most difficult category in the whole antique business to advise on. Precious or semi-precious stones, glass, crystal, precious or semi-precious metal, weight of stones, weight of metal, cut, composition, clarity, type of setting, design — on and on and on the variables go. It's as if antique jewelry is on a personality binge all by itself!

So what does it require to become an antique jewelry expert, other than knowing weights, type of stone, and metal composition? Experience, and tons of it, that's what.

Experience, resulting in firsthand knowledge, is what distinguishes a successful antique jewelry dealer from the myriad that constantly fall by the wayside. And this experience can only be gained with time. Being able to distinguish real precious stones from excellent fakes, what settings are popular, what's in vogue, and most importantly, what prices are doing in the market, is what distinguishes a successful dealer in this most complex of antique categories.

These experts were all once amateurs, too — so it's not impossible. Difficult yes, impossible no. Let's begin with some things antique jewelry has in common with other antique categories.

What is Antique Jewelry?

As with all antiques, antique jewelry over 100 years old is considered truly antique. For U.S. Customs purposes this means that it can be imported duty-free. For those purchasing very expensive antique jewelry, it means that they have a genuine antique and not just one called so at the whim of the dealer. A good provenance is essential for such purposes since values vary depending on history and previous ownership, especially with valuable pieces.

The best way to explain antique jewelry is to answer a series of the most frequently asked questions. As previously mentioned, this explanation will blur precious and costume jewelry together but explanations and answers will emphasize this when necessary.

Question: Is there any way to define the different types and designs of antique jewelry?
Answer: Yes. Antique jewelry, particularly that from England, is classified by the same Royalty periods used in furniture, silver, and ceramics. In jewelry, however, two other design styles are used as designations, namely Art Nouveau and Art Deco. In addition, the terms Retro, Period, and Collectible are also used to indicate period or desirability. For clarification, here they are again.

Is costume jewelry valuable?

Georgian: The period 1720 to 1820 covering the reign of the four King Georges. Used to date English jewelry, but also identifies the same design styles in other countries.

Victorian: Refers to the 1837 to 1901 Queen Victoria period in the case of English jewelry. Also used to identify style of jewelry produced in other countries while not implying that the jewelry was English-made.

Edwardian: Covers the 1905 to 1920 King Edward period when delicate designs in platinum and diamonds were the trend.

Art Nouveau: An 1890 to 1915 style of jewelry with flowing lines, floral decorations, beautiful nude women and fantasy nature creations. Considered artistic rather than pretty or attractive.

Art Deco: Bold, modern designs with sharp lines and clashing color combinations inspired by the 1920 to 1930 French "Art Decoratif" movement.

Period Jewelry: Categorized by a particular style and craftsman quality, period jewelry can be genuinely antique (over 100 years old), or otherwise.

Collectible Jewelry: Usually refers to a particular artist's jewelry with its own customer following. Not necessarily stylish, precious, or antique, it is called collectible due to its desirability from a large following.

Retro Jewelry: A large and heavy design of jewelry produced in the 1940s and 1950s often using rubies and diamonds in a "rose" gold setting. Very popular during those years, it retains a substantial following due to price rises governed by the weight and size of its precious stones.

So you know the piece's period. How much is it worth?

Question: What is "Costume" jewelry and is it valuable?
Answer: 1. Costume jewelry may be antique, period, or contemporary, but it is all made with non-precious metals and synthetic or glass stones. 2. Victorian costume jewelry is sought after due to its complex and pretty designs combining different colors of glass.

Estate jewelry.

3. Costume jewelry's value depends on its maker. Pieces manufactured by Haskel, Hobe, and Chanel fetch three- and four-figure prices. 4. Lesser known makes are worth as little as $10, but all styles and designs have a considerable collector following.

An antique beginner interested in jewelry will also hear the terms Revival, Reproduction and Fake used in the day-to-day business chat. These terms mean the following:

Revival: A piece of jewelry incorporating previous era designs modified to interpret them in a different artistic fashion. Most "revival" jewelry pieces are genuinely more than 100 years old and are very collectible.

Reproduction: A modern copy. Although some reproductions are over fifty years old and very difficult to distinguish from the real thing.

Fake: A fraudulent piece of jewelry designed to fool the buyer into thinking it's the real thing. Some are very difficult to detect and can fool even experts.

Question: What is "Estate" jewelry?
Answer: Originally used by auctioneers to fool buyers into thinking that products sold from an old home are more authentically antique, the use of the term "Estate jewelry" is a smoke screen that means nothing.

An amateur should bear in mind that estate sale antiques are no more authentic than those in auctions. Auctioneers tend to use such terms to gloss over the fact that much of the merchandise in an estate sale is really just old household junk. If you know your jewelry business, check pieces of interest thoroughly, and ignore the sales hype.

Question: How is antique jewelry valued?
Answer: Starting with the weight of the metal, the weight or size of the stones, and the type of design used, the dealer establishes a ball park figure on any specific piece by researching the price of equivalent items. For the individual owner that isn't so easy.

Using an expert appraiser will speed the process up but they charge heavily for their services. It will also depend on the reason for requiring the valuation. To establish a sale price one has to remember that most retail prices are double the purchase price. If the valuation is required for insurance purposes, the owner will have to consider the replacement cost which could be considerably higher.

From the above you can see that jewelry valuation is a very inexact science at best. My suggestion is that you research equivalent pieces and then make your own realistic judgment call.

An unmarked gold nugget.

Nothing replaces knowledge gained through experience. Browse the malls, go to jewelry auctions, look up research books and talk to the experts and pick their brains. That way you'll pick up tips and build knowledge.

Question: If the gold in my jewelry is unmarked, does that mean it is worthless?
Answer: Not necessarily. A lot of old gold jewelry was unstamped or stamped with obscure markings that no one can decipher. Stamping wasn't mandated in the U.S. until the early 1900s and lots of antique pieces were unstamped. Gold quality cannot be determined just by weight but requires testing to establish karat purity. Antique gold is particularly hard to type.

Question: How does a piece of jewelry's history impact its value?
Answer: Provenance, or the item's history established through sales or other record keeping, has a major effect on the price of a piece of jewelry. Historic jewelry with an impressive provenance usually means the piece will attain an impressive sale price in a top notch auction while no provenance, or a questionable one, makes a desirable piece more difficult to sell. An antique beginner should not pay high prices for jewelry without a good provenance and I would suggest that you concentrate on family jewelry that has been handed down through generations.

I must mention condition again. As important as provenance, the condition of the jewelry will be the determining factor in its sale price. Make sure that clasps are working, that claws holding the stones are tight and that pins don't drop off. Clean the jewelry in warm, soapy water and dry with soft tissue or cloth before showing it to a client. The glitter of gold and the sparkle of diamonds is worth at least 10 percent extra.

Question: What does the "karat" in gold mean?
Answer: The karat refers to the quality or purity of gold (no alloys mixed in). Pure gold is designated 24K, while 18K means 18 parts out of 24, or 75 percent, are pure gold, 14K is 14 parts out of 24 or 58.5 percent. Because pure gold is too soft for jewelry purposes almost all gold jewelry is less then 24K due to the addition of harder metals.

An appraiser's report. There is no standard or qualification required for someone to call themself an appraiser.

Unfortunately there is no universal standard for gold stamping, so many countries have their own. European countries with a decimal system, for example, use 1,000 parts instead of 24K to indicate 100 percent purity. Therefore, 18K gold under this system is 750 parts and so on down.

An expert may be able to establish value, but how do you find an expert? When asked to refer one I always suggest that the person look in the yellow pages. This is because there is no standard or qualification required for someone to call themself an appraiser. Furthermore, the antique business is so diverse and complicated that a furniture appraiser may know nothing at all about antique jewelry. The more reputable ones, however, usually belong to an association and my suggestion is that you avoid ones who don't. Nationally recognized appraiser associations exist in the United States, and I would recommend that you ask them to refer someone or to give you a list of their members if you require the services of an antique appraiser.

Question: Why is antique jewelry more difficult to repair?

Answer: The gold in antique jewelry is usually 18K and, therefore, softer to work with. Since heat is required to make it malleable, many jewelers don't wish to take on the responsibility of damaging what may be an old family heirloom, particularly as replacement parts may be impossible to obtain. Restoration of old pieces is also time consuming and requires techniques that the jeweler may not know. Stones cut to antique designs may not be readily available and many jewelers don't want to get into a situation where they have to admit that they can't help you.

That's one reason why a beginner should not buy antique jewelry that is damaged in even the slightest way. Just remember that the dealer offering you this bargain knows that to repair the piece is very expensive or even impossible. Such a thing happened to me with a solid gold Omega watch that even the factory in Switzerland couldn't repair due to a lack of parts. It's the old story, isn't it? If it looks too good to be true, it probably is.

Question: Why is an "old cut" diamond in antique jewelry not worth as much as a more "modern" cut?

Answer: This is total nonsense and is used by crafty diamond dealers to push down the price of even the most desirable diamonds. The valuation of diamonds is based on the Four C's — carat, clarity, cut and color. The combination of these — the

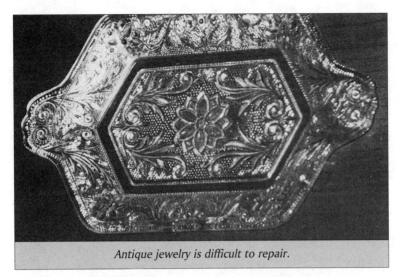

Antique jewelry is difficult to repair.

strength of one to the other, the color thrown up by the facets, the fault lines of the stone, etc., etc. — determine value. An old cut means nothing except that the cuts are bold, and if someone tells you that it may need to be re-cut and thus be reduced in size, tell them to take a hike! Over one carat, good clarity, and excellent color determines 80 percent of the price. An "old" cut even enhances this.

Question: What is a "Rose-cut" diamond?
Answer: A rose-cut is a much cruder cut than is common today and refers to an antique faceting style used when tools were not so high-tech. It means that the diamond ends up with a flat base and fewer facets. The rose-cut does cause the diamond to sparkle, but not as brilliantly as the finer cuts of today. It has a more subtle look and antique jewelry with rose-cut, high quality diamonds is sought by collectors world-wide because of its rarity. Such antique jewelry is often set in silver, and finding a large diamond (over one carat) with such a cut is a find indeed!

Question: Why are smaller "Rose-cut" diamonds sometimes referred to as "Marcasite"?
Answer: To call them such is totally wrong. Marcasites are iron pyrite, which was popular in cheaper jewelry during the 1920s. Because the cruder rose-cut was used in small diamonds, some dealers mistake them for Marcasite. Unscrupulous dealers also call smaller diamonds Marcasite to pay next to nothing for them. Marcasite jewelry is collectible, particularly if set in silver.

While on the subject of stones and the cruder cuts, let's discuss some other items and terms used in antique jewelry.

Question: What is the meaning of "Cameo"?
Answer: Cameo means the carving is a raised profile design above the surface.

Question: What is "Intaglio"?
Answer: Intaglio means the carving is below the surface of the stone — the opposite of cameo.

Cameo means the carving is a raised profile design.

Pearl Jewelry

Antique jewelry uses many stones, and oftentimes these are pearls. There seems to be a lot of confusion about the difference between cultured and real pearls. Real pearls are nature grown and harvested by Japanese women divers, though this method is now almost dead. Cultured pearls are grown on farms by inserting the chip of an oyster shell into the living oyster. Covering the chip with a few millimeters of its secretion, the growing oyster forms a hard pearl cover which takes anywhere from three to five years to complete. Almost all cultured pearl production comes from Japan, but some freshwater pearl culture is now taking place in America's southern states.

Antique jewelry with genuine pearls is increasingly valuable, and for the very reason detailed above, the supply of real pearls is limited. In April 1998, there was even a rumor that disease had infested the Japanese pearl beds and as a result prices shot through the roof. Amateur buyers often forget that real pearls are not as perfectly formed as cultured pearls. This makes them more valuable rather than the opposite, which seems to be a popular misconception. Real pearls require X-raying to confirm that they are truly real, though a few experts can tell the difference by eye. You are not likely to encounter such an expert in the everyday antique business, so if anyone tells you they can tell such a difference, don't believe them.

When discussing antiques with strangers I am often asked if I have any tips for finding bargains. Usually, women who are interested in antique jewelry have the questions. My answer is always the same: "Find items in some old, dusty attic to get a bargain. It's unlikely it will be jewelry, though."

The plain fact is that antique jewelry is usually treasured by its owners and very few really valuable items ever enter the market at a bargain price. Unlike furniture, which is often stuffed away in some dusty corner and just looks like old junk, jewelry always conjures up visions of wealth. As such it is kept in the forefront of anyone's estate.

Solid silver. Find items in some dusty attic to get a bargain.

Precious Jewelry

Who knows how diamonds are weighed, what the difference between 14 and 18 karat gold is, or what color emeralds are? Probably most of us. But how about settings? How much do we know about them? Very little, I bet! And how about clarity, cut and color?

Before a beginner gets involved in buying and selling precious jewelry, I recommend they spend considerable time becoming knowledgeable. Find a dealer who will exchange knowledge for part time work is my best advice. Learn as much as you can about, rubies, emeralds, opals, claw settings and clasps before launching out on your own. Then and only then start dealing — very slowly and carefully. To be really knowledgeable in precious jewelry you need lots of experience which exposes you to all its nuances.

Costume Jewelry

Costume jewelry is without question a good category for the beginner. Victorian and Edwardian pieces are plentiful and worth dealing in. At prices from $10 and up, customers buy the jewelry because it catches their eye. To illustrate my point, here is a story of my own about costume jewelry:

A few years back I was on an antique buying trip in England. One Saturday afternoon I found myself at Jacob's Market, an antique center in Cardiff, Wales. Wandering around the tables I spied a rattan basket full of costume jewelry. There must have been 150 pieces of all shapes, sizes, and color combinations. Rings, pins, bracelets — everything was there, with each piece marked at anywhere from 5 pounds ($8) to 20 pounds ($35). In a flash of impetuousness I went up to the dealer and offered her $500 for the lot, take it or leave it. Guess what she did on a slow Saturday afternoon?

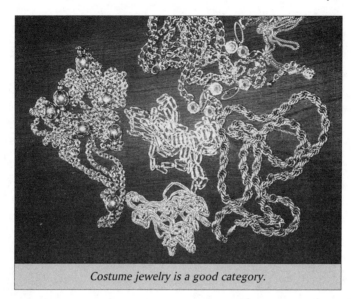

Costume jewelry is a good category.

Two weeks later I marked each piece from $10 for the cheapest rings to $70 for the best pins and set them out in my store. Six weeks later I had sold the lot for a total of $2,000 plus, plus!

That's the way to do it. As an amateur you can't go wrong with Victorian costume jewelry, then you can work your way up to precious jewelry as your knowledge grows. Anyone can afford costume jewelry at $10 to $20 for a piece, but not many people can spend $2,000 on one precious stone.

Miscellaneous Jewelry

Jewelry doesn't just mean rings, bracelets and pins. It also means jewelry boxes, cigarette boxes, snuff boxes, pocket watches, jeweled pill boxes, bejeweled combs and brushes and enameled pendants. These items also require specialized knowledge, and I would recommend that you begin with smaller items like pill boxes. You might just pick one up to find that the glass decorations that the owner thought were worthless are in fact genuine precious stones. It happened to me once. I bought a pair of small, hallmarked silver buckles with what the dealer said were red glass decorations. On instinct I took them to a jeweler in Grapevine, Texas. After examination he confirmed them as small, but terrific rubies. You can never tell when you'll get lucky in the antiques business!

Here are a few words bandied about by jewelry dealers.

Vinaigrette: No, not the salad dressing! When used by antique dealers it means a small decorative bottle or container with a perforated top for holding things like rings or smelling salts.

Baguette: A gem cut into a long narrow rectangle.

Chalcedony: A translucent or transparent milky or grayish quartz with crystals arranged in parallel bands.

Antique jewelry box.

Cabochon: A highly polished, convex-cut, non-faceted gem or style of cutting.

Lapis lazuli: An opaque azure-blue or deep blue lazulite gemstone.

Riviere: A necklace of precious stones in one string.

Pave diamonds: Chips or very small stones.

Here are some diamond terms:

Inclusion: Fault or marking.

Pinpoints: Crystals that are transparent, opaque or carbon.

Clouds: Groups of pinpoints.

Feathers: Fractures.

Recommendation: Amateurs beware! The precious antique jewelry field requires expertise. Despite this, here are items that are worth looking for.

> $1,500 and under — Victorian jewelry is recommended as are men's gold cufflinks and tie pins.
>
> $1,500 to $5,000 — Excellent color solitaire rings are bargains, particularly more than 1.5 carats.
>
> $5,000 and more — Three to seven carat diamonds, Faberge jewelry, and antique diamond rivieres are all excellent buys at any price.

Summary

Antique jewelry is a complex category with many factors that affect price, not least of which is preference. It's an expensive category, and is not recommended for the beginner unless one begins with Victorian costume jewelry.

Antique jewelry is fun but requires a cautious approach. I do, however, recommend it, as it is both an enjoyable and profitable business for those who take the time to build a specialized knowledge in this area.

Chapter Seven

Commemorative Memorabilia

Commemorative antiques cover many products.

Commemorative antiques cover many product lines — pottery, silver, pendant jewelry and pop art, among other things. The category is almost more collectible-based than it is necessarily commemorative. Commemorative posters of musical events along with ceramic plates, silver tankards and Andy Warhol paintings all contribute and make this a very interesting category indeed. Diversity permits opportunity and therefore makes this a definite product line for antique beginners. If you can't find something that interests you among the commemorative items, then you won't find anything anywhere!

Before discussing the various segments that comprise this highly interesting classification, I would like to reiterate something that I have said before that is even more important in this product category: condition of the item is everything!

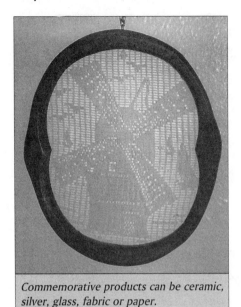

Commemorative products can be ceramic, silver, glass, fabric or paper.

Busts are popular.

Unlike antique furniture where the condition can be improved, the condition of commemorative plates, posters, Disney postcards and a whole host of delicate products included in this category can't. Furniture can be cleaned, polished with wax to bring out the patina and the screws tightened. Once coffee-stained, a poster of Disney's "Pluto and a Cat" is damaged beyond repair. The stain is ingrained into the paper forever. More importantly, the stain will probably reduce the poster's value by more than 50 percent. By telling you this particular poster, printed in 1940, is worth $5,000 in mint condition, you can understand just how much money I'm talking about.

Most commemorative products are collectibles. As such they appreciate over time. Collectibles are also subject to fashion trends, which should be born in mind when buying and selling. The buy low, sell high philosophy is even more important here, though collectibles are almost sure to increase in value over the long haul. One other aspect a beginner should remember about commemorative products is that they are bought by very enthusiastic collectors. This means that a beginner should be as knowledgeable as possible before venturing into the marketplace. Selecting according to your particular interest and learning as much as you can about it before clashing horns with an expert dealer is not a bad idea.

Commemorative products come from England (royalty and royal occasions), the United States (historic dates, presidents, events and entertainment) and from the continent (usually famous people). Made in ceramic, silver, glass, fabric and paper they cover every material possible. Since most people have seen commemorative English pottery depicting royal personalities such as Queen Victoria and Princes Di, let's start with those, shall we?

Busts form a valuable part of commemoratives.

Pottery: British commemorative pottery is the world's best known. Plates, mugs, jugs and busts are all very popular. The blue-dash chargers of the late 17th century with Royalist themes are some of the earliest products available to collectors. As covered in the chapter on ceramics, blue delft is highly sought after with Queen Anne or George I items topping the list. Although commemorative themes such as the 19th century opening of the Manchester and Liverpool Railway line are sought after, it is items with portraits of the various Dukes, such as the Duke of Marlborough, that command high prices. Those that depict royal personages such as King William IV, Edward VIII, Queen Caroline, Princess Charlotte, and of course Queen Victoria are also up there. Rarity is the critical factor, with the most rare items fetching prices of $1,000 or more. While on the subject of Queen Victoria, the 19th century saw a glut of Queen Victoria products and these must be in perfect condition to generate any interest among buyers.

British commemorative pottery was manufactured by all the well known names. Royal Doulton, Spode and Staffordshire potteries all produced various items with interesting themes. A loving cup, color-enameled with a portrait of Edward VIII flanked by crusaders, Britannia, ships, and an elaborate coat-of-arms is typical of the complex designs used. This cup would be worth close to $2,000 on the open market in 1999.

For the beginner British commemorative pottery is an excellent product line. With so many shapes and themes available, it also provides a terrific history lesson.

Commemorative busts: Although they're not as popular as plates and jugs, busts nevertheless form a valuable part of the commemorative antique business. Busts of 18th century Queen Victoria, Alexander I of Russia, Milton and Plato are desirable. The more highly colored and enameled, the more valuable they are. Many have gilt as a desirable feature. Enoch Wood was a particularly good artist in the early 18th century and his busts fetch high prices on the London antique market. Copeland's Parian bust of Juno, modeled by W. Theed, is also the type of bust that sells for well over $8,000.

Plaques: Few of these can be found but they are worth collecting. Many battle scenes are depicted on commemorative plaques. Battleships such as the Duke of Wellington, which boasted 131 cannons and was one of the largest 'Man o' War' ships in the British fleet, are popular subjects.

Porcelain boxes: Snuff and jewelry boxes are the mainstay of the commemorative niche. Many such products have important horse-mounted figures and often depict hunting scenes. Antique beginners should ensure that edges, particularly those of the lids, aren't chipped.

Coats of arms: The Goss China factory produced high-quality crested china between 1858 and 1939 in three periods. The first, from 1858 to1887 is famous for parian busts and ornamental ware. The second, from 1881 to 1934, produced Heraldic designs. The third period, from 1929 to 1939, is known for colored pottery.

Ceramic items and pottery with Heraldic or royal coats of arms are very popular in the U.S., particularly since the history of these can be traced back to the medieval times. Many related souvenir items were produced, but when World War I began in 1914, demand for crested china fell. Then, military souvenirs were produced until 1930, when overall sales ground to a halt. Fortunately, vast amounts of product had already been produced. Goss china is an inexpensive line for the amateur and the large variety of items means there is a ready supply. Plus, most items are likely to appreciate due to the cessation of production.

Commemorative sports items: There isn't much interest in British commemorative items in the U.S., although they fetch high prices in Europe. Football jerseys, cricket caps, commemorative postal covers and emblems all go for $3,000 to $5,000 in England. If you find such an item, I suggest you purchase it, send it to an English auction house and pay off your mortgage!

American sports items tend to come from the more modern sports but these are still very collectible. Sports cards of every type are a specialized section as are World Series programs. My suggestion to the antique beginner is to also collect old leather football helmets, boots, basketballs and baseball bats, as these are sure to appreciate with time. I believe golf collectibles will also become a separate segment that is bound to grow in importance.

Commemorative pendants: A real surprise, painted and enameled pendants fetch huge prices. For example, a "Military Officer" 1788 commemorative pendant sold for $25,000 recently at a London auction. Many pendants commemorating important women of the 17th century are worth at least $5,000. Some names to look for are Richard Schwager (1868), John Smart (1788), Jeramiah Meyer (1735-1789), Abraham Daniel (1805) and William Grimaldi (1751-1830).

Many commemorative pendants are made from silver gilt and most are enameled. Extremely small (around three inches high) they are very rare. Most are signed and dated on the back. Too expensive for the amateur, pendants are a commemorative surprise. If you find one and the price is reasonable, grab it.

Movie commemoratives: There is a terrific demand for movie commemoratives, especially recently. Posters, lobby cards, working scripts, props and celluloids are just

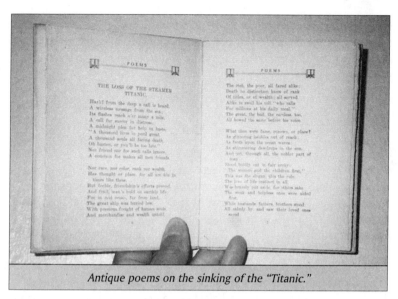

Antique poems on the sinking of the "Titanic."

a few of the items in demand. A "Thing Box" from the 1964-66 "Addams Family" TV series is typical. Together with four photographs and a letter from Jackie Coogan, it is worth more than $25,000 at auction today. In 1964 it was worth less than $50. Another example is a 1936 poster for the movie "The Oregon Trail" starring John Wayne. When released by Republic Pictures the poster couldn't have been worth more than a few dollars and yet it is estimated it's worth at least $15,000 today. Movie props have also skyrocketed in price and are expected to continue to do so as computer animation takes over some of the physical requirements involved with making a movie.

Speaking of movies, I saw a news item in the English "Express" newspaper about two slips of paper that recorded the SOS messages from the Titanic as it was sinking. Hand written by the radio operator on the nearby ship, Virginia, the messages were received on the night the Titanic went down, April 1912. The first slip of paper records the message: "Have struck iceberg and require immediate assistance." The second records, "Sinking. We are putting passengers off on small lifeboats."

Both of these originally handwritten slips of paper came up for auction at Christie's on May 14, 1998, and after furious bidding fetched more than $5,000 for the pair. Just imagine! A movie spawning enough attention that someone would pay that much money for two pieces of brown paper.

For the beginner, I would highly recommend movie memorabilia. Signed postcards of Charlie Chaplin, Laurel and Hardy, and even recent plaster portraits of Christopher Reeves as Superman are desirable.

While on the subject of movie memorabilia, I must mention a story that appeared in "The New York Times" on May 15, 1998. Although strictly art, it can also be considered memorabilia due to the fact that it involved Marilyn Monroe, whose commemorative items are in huge demand.

On May 14, an iconic painting of Marilyn Monroe termed "Orange Marilyn" by Andy Warhol sold at Sotheby's for $17.3 million. This was four times more than any

Terrific opportunities exist in this category.

Andy Warhol painting had ever sold for before and can be attributed to the subject matter. The reason for such a high price was because of the painting's provenance (there it is again). It was being sold by a descendant of Karl Stroeher of Darmstadt, Germany, whose collection of 20th century works was the first in Europe to include American Pop Art.

It's also interesting that the previous record for a Warhol was set in 1989 when Christies sold another painting of Marilyn Monroe called "Shot Red Marilyn." It was named so for the damage it sustained in 1964 when a woman entered Warhol's Manhattan studio, aimed a gun at his head, missed, and hit several paintings on the floor, among which was this particular painting of the famous film star.

Pop commemoratives: Pop ephemera is growing rapidly as an antique commemorative due to the larger-than-life lifestyles of the Beatles, Elvis, Marvin Gaye, Mick Jagger, Michael Jackson and Jimi Hendrix. Posters, autographed slips of paper, and signed covers are all gaining popularity. Also, funky clothes such as a Jimi Hendrix velvet stage jacket decorated at the shoulders with embroidered orange, yellow, and green flower heads and mirrored sequins are highly desirable. Some items, such as a complete stage outfit from Prince's Purple Rain Tour of 1984, are worth as much as $20,000.

Probably the most recognizable pop memorabilia item is Michael Jackson's rhinestone glove. Printed with the artist's name and a Western Costume Co., Hollywood label woven into the edge, Jackson wore it at the 1984 Grammy Award ceremonies on Feb. 28, 1984 — the night he walked away with eight Grammies. He also wore it to the "USA For Africa — We Are The World" recording sessions on Jan. 28, 1985. Worth at least $50,000, that glove will reach over $100,000 at auction should it be sold in the next few years. The most curious fact about this glove is that it turns the meaning of "antique" upside-down. Only sixteen years old, and it is already a classic. What it might be worth 100 years from now is mind boggling.

Disney commemoratives and memorabilia defy description.

And if that isn't enough, Michael Jackson's sequined jacket is also setting records. Black, with matching lining, gold-colored buttons decorated with the American eagle, and with the right shoulder embellished with a chain and black studded leather strap, the jacket is a commemorative worth at least $30,000 on today's market.

Before moving on from pop memorabilia, I have to mention the artist formerly known as "Prince." During the Purple Rain Tour of 1984 he wore an outfit that consisted of an ornate black crepe coat with pink and brown net overlay, a pair of matching high-waisted stretch pants, a pair of high-heeled ankle boots and a white ruffled shirt with a "Prince" label. This outfit is now valued at close to $30,000 on the antique market, and if it ever comes up for auction it will probably fetch twice that.

In reviewing pop commemoratives and memorabilia I can only advise the amateur antiquer to go for it. Terrific opportunities exist in this category as many posters and items are stuck away in some dusty attic. It is definitely a very fast-growing segment of the antique business and will continue to be.

I am now going to give you a really hot tip that will make you a fortune if you can find any of the items I am about to mention. Don't ever say I didn't look out for my readers.

The Wallace and Gromit characters immortalized on film by the Oscar winning animation company Aardman (http://www.aardman.com) are really hot. Limited, hand-painted sculptures of the lovable pair are going to be very, very, valuable in the future. With Wallace and Gromit memorabilia going global, if you can find early products buy them up for goodness sake.

By the way, if you find these items and don't want them, get hold of me via the publisher, please!

Of the many movie commemorative items, Disney movie memorabilia has the biggest following.

Disneyana: Often labeled as "ephemera" meaning "lasting a short time," Disney commemorative material and memorabilia items defy that description. It may be the child in all of us hankering after the simpler life that makes them so.

Most of the famous Disney movies are animated, so it's not surprising that Disney commemoratives and memorabilia consist of sketches from famous movies like "Snow White and the Seven Dwarfs" and "Peter Pan." Illustrated premiere programs are also collectibles as are celluloids and cards signed by Walt Disney himself. Although of recent 1955 vintage, sketches such as those of "Lady" in a muzzle, "Jock" glaring, and "Mickey and Minnie Mouse" sell for prices as high as $5,000 apiece. A great antique for the amateur, Disney commemoratives will continue to be in high demand.

Militaria

While on the subject of commemoratives, I must mention militaria items that are used in movies. These will be discussed in a later chapter on that subject. Items like brooches, Chains of Order and badges used in war movies are now considered commemorative. Such items are difficult to find but are very worthwhile if and when they do come to market.

Commemorative glass: While not as prolific as ceramics, commemorative glass is highly collectible. Many pieces are of continental origin but 19th century English decanters with portraits of Field Marshall Duke of Wellington and Lord Nelson are occasionally found. Commemorative rummers, engraved with sailing ships and Nelson's catafalque are also occasionally found, but due to the scarcity of product on the antique market, glass is not recommended for the antique beginner.

Commemorating a hunt—very fascinating.

An extremely varied antique class, commemorative and memorabilia items are highly fascinating. Here are some words commonly used when describing such items.

Chargers: A large shallow dish or platter. The shape was perfect for portraits.

Blue-dash: Stark, all-blue decoration much like blue willow.

Parian: A stark white pottery associated with Belleek and Irish manufacturers.

Celluloid: A colorless, flammable material made from nitrocellulose and camphor.

Goss china: A particular type of specialized, crested product line made by the English Goss factory.

Pearlware: Pottery first made by Wedgewood in 1779 containing soap rock and cobalt oxide, which produces a white color.

Commemorating the first sale.

Fifteen-hundred dollars and less — Disney memorabilia.

Cartouche: A scroll-surrounded space provided for an inscription. Can also be an oval or oblong figure in ancient Egyptian hieroglyphics that encloses characters listing the name of epithets of royal or divine personages.

Union motif: A flag motif.

Quimper: A particular style of porcelain from the Quimper region of France.

Faience: Earthenware decorated with colorful, opaque glazes, often a moderate greenish blue.

Recommendation: Commemoratives and memorabilia are both good antique areas for the beginner. The wide range of interesting products and their availability enable you to start with a modest investment that is sure to appreciate. My recommendation is:

$1,500 and under — Chargers with the unusual Victorian portraits and movie memorabilia, particularly Disney.

$1,500 to $5,000 — Pop memorabilia, particularly clothing.

$5,000 and more — I would suggest that you get hold of guitars and musical instruments belonging to top pop stars and bands. Concentrate only on those that are really popular, like the Rolling Stones.

Commemorative items and memorabilia antiques are still in the process of developing into new product lines and if you can get in at the bottom of this type of collecting, you will cash in down the line. This is particularly true for younger collectors who are more familiar with the various pop groups.

A baby's blanket — commemorative antiques are still pioneering new product lines.

Chapter Eight

Toys, Dolls, Teddy Bears and Much, Much More

Toys are wonderful antique products.

Toys are wonderful antique products. They span the whole gamut of playthings that remind us of those wonderful days before the age of plastics. Terrific items for the antique beginner, they offer a wide variety and there seems to be something for everyone.

So what items fall under the category of antique toys? Two of the biggest categories are dolls and teddy bears. Trains, money banks, tin plate and many other miscellaneous products such as rocking chairs also fill this interesting antique category. What is most fun about these products is that most still work and can be played with as they were so many years ago.

Carved wooden, wax, cloth, celluloid, and bisque dolls vie for prominence in this crowded field.

Antique dolls are valued by their material composition, country of origin, and by who made them.

Dolls

When most people think of dolls they think of them as fairly simple products. A bit of cloth, some porcelain and a wad of stuffing — that's all that dolls are, right?

Wrong! And certainly antique dolls aren't.

Carved wooden dolls, wax dolls, wax-over composition dolls, cloth dolls, celluloid dolls and Bisque dolls all vie for prominence in this crowded category. And many of them require an extremely fat checkbook if you want to become their proud owner.

A number of major factors affect antique doll prices besides, of course, condition. They are rare marks, labels, and original boxes. This is particularly true with Barbie dolls that are now becoming so collectible. Even the famous auction house Christie's has organized a special auction for them. What is amazing about antique dolls is that when really rare antique ones come up for sale, they very often do so with their original packing in pristine condition. This shows that many are collected for investment purposes only as they certainly don't appear to have been played with or handled roughly.

Antique dolls are valued by their material composition, their country of origin, and by what specialist manufacturer made them. Since material composition is the most important of these, I will start by detailing the various materials used. Also, keep in mind that collections of dolls have a higher value than single dolls, as is true of most antiques. The way the dolls are dressed is also a major factor in valuing a doll and those with authentic national costumes are much sought after.

Let's cover the materials used, shall we?

If dolls interest you, ask for the address of a local doll association.

Wooden dolls: German, English, Swiss and French manufacturers predominate, with some wooden dolls dating as far back as the late 1700s. American manufactured dolls are also popular, especially those that are copies of famous personalities.

Antique wooden dolls come either carved totally in wood (with some even having jointed limbs), or in a combination of cloth and wood. Many are made with a combination of many materials — porcelain, cloth and wood are popular mediums, with the odd bit of glass thrown in for good measure. What is so interesting about many wooden dolls is how intricate the carvings are. Detailed features, complete with wrinkles and expressions are not unusual. One set of German dolls I once saw even had their lower jaws hinged so that their mouths could open and close.

Georgian period wooden dolls predominate among English antiques with some having interesting provenance. One George III wooden doll, reputed to have belonged to Queen Victoria, had painted features, inserted blue eyes with dotted lashes, white real, blonde hair, squared hips peg jointed to long tapering legs with block feet, cloth upper arms with blue kid forearms, and wore a pink, beige silk dress. This doll's provenance indicates that the Queen gave it to her lady in waiting, the Honorable Caroline Cavandish, who then gave it to the aunt of the present owner. Whew! Now you can see what I mean by complicated manufacture and detailed provenance all rolled into one. Incidentally that doll is worth nearly $6,000.

Among continental dolls, those by Grodnetal set the standard. With painted features and jointed limbs, these circa 1800s wooden dolls come dressed in both German and other national costumes. Commercial production of dolls in this Alpine Thuringian Forest and Ore mountain area of Grodnetal started in the 16th century when carving and wood turning became an extensive cottage industry. Not only did they use solid wood, but papier-mâché was often used for dolls' heads. Many of the famous Grodnetal dolls were sold out of the city of Nuremberg and are often referred to by this name rather than Grodnetal. A beginner buying such dolls as collector's items, or as an investment, would be well advised to ensure that the provenance goes back to the 1800s.

Dolls traced back to their manufacturer increase in value dramatically.

Male and female dolls in pairs are valuable.

Wooden antique dolls are an excellent product for the beginner, and doll shows, antique doll sales, and even auctions are conducted on a regular basis. If dolls interest you, go to the nearest doll shop and ask the owner for the address of a local doll association. I also recommend that you gain as much knowledge as you can by talking to enthusiasts at one of your area doll shows. Such enthusiasts are always prepared to discuss their life's passion.

Wax dolls: Poured wax or wax shaped over a composition? Which is best? Doesn't matter. Wax dolls, which were overlooked in the past, have suddenly become popular — especially those in original clothing and in good condition. Whether they're 18th or 19th century doesn't matter, either. Both periods are in. Look for the shop markings, which determine originality. The importance of this is illustrated by the story of an English lady who took her doll to an appraiser only to be told it was worth virtually nothing. She added it to her garage sale and sold it to her neighbor for $30. The neighbor searched the doll's body and found a hitherto unknown stamp. She researched it and it turned out to be that of a fancy Sloane Street, London jeweler known to have been in business from 1886 to 1908. This doll then sold at auction for more than $2,000. Apparently the neighbor shared her good fortune with her friend so the story had a happy ending. That's not always the case, though, is it?

English wax dolls can often be traced back to their manufacturer and, if they are, their value increases dramatically. Well known names like Pierotti, Charles Marsh, fancy Belgravia Square, London jeweler and importer William J. Weeden, and Fleishmann and Bodel are the ones you should look for. Pierotti, in particular, is highly sought after and

The advent of bisque enabled a far greater range.

This 32-inch doll looks alive.

even many of his damaged dolls fetch prices of more than $800. Incidentally, you may wonder how an Italian name became associated with English doll making. The fact is that many Italians settled in London in the 1850s and brought with them their skills, which they soon put to use in businesses located in their newly adopted home.

Pairs of wax dolls occasionally come up for sale and these are definitely worth purchasing, particularly if they reflect male and female period costumes. I once saw a pair of wax-over composition, 18th century costumed dolls sell for more than $2,000. The male doll was dressed in black, silk knee britches, red velvet, a silver braided jacket, tricorn hat and heeled shoes. The female partner doll was dressed in ruby pleated silk skirt with floral overdress trimmed with lace, heeled shoes, and she was carrying a fan. Both dolls had blue eyes, blond mohair wigs, stuffed bodies, waxed arms and composition lower legs. The female even had an open mouth with perfect teeth showing.

Since prices for wax and wax-over composition dolls vary from about $500 to $2,500, they are a good bet for amateur collectors as they are sure to appreciate in value. Don't forget — markings and condition govern price.

Bisque dolls: Bisque dolls are the largest and most valuable category of antique dolls. Although the British made some bisque dolls — Staffordshire porcelain especially — it was the German manufacturers who were the masters, and were renowned for their expertise. As usual, the French were not far behind their European compatriots and in many cases manufacturers like Francois Gaultier and Jumeau were even ahead.

The advent of bisque in doll manufacture enabled craftsmen to make a far greater range of characters, and this class includes everything from baby dolls to small accessory bisque people. The bisque period (1850 to 1930) was definitely the golden age of doll manufacturing. With bisque colors ranging from a moderate yellowish pink to grayish yellow, all sorts of jester dolls, Father Christmas dolls, and Oriental character dolls crowd this doll segment. It is the exquisite female faces and detailed period costumed dolls, however, that fetch prices as high as $20,000. One such doll, made by Jumeau in 1875, is an example. With its fixed brown glass, paperweight eyes, pierced ears with earrings, real brown hair over cork plate, jointed wood and composite body and, wearing a pink dress and quizzical expression, this 32-inch doll looks like it is alive. Apart from its incredibly lifelike appearance, the authenticated Jumeau stamp also pushed its price up to record levels.

Something worth mentioning is that many dolls come with accessories. These should always remain with the original piece for price appreciation reasons and should not be sold separately even if you are offered a decent price.

Since bisque dolls are such an important category of antique dolls, here are a few of the better known producers.

Jumeau: France. 1842 to 1899. Detailed features such as plump cheeks, strong, thin eyebrows, large expression-filled eyes and detailed costumes characterized Jumeau dolls. The most famous doll maker of the 19th century, Le Maison Jumeau (House of Jumeau) was founded in 1845 by Pierre Jumeau, whose dolls were quiet and mystical. Succeeded by his son Emile-Louis, whose own dolls were healthy and cheerful, the business continued until Emile-Louis' death in 1899. Because of their expressive faces, Jumeau dolls tend to be labeled based on their expressions. For instance, "Long Faced" or "Bebe Trieste." The most famous of their dolls was "Bebe Jumeau," made by Emile-Louis in 1895. Twenty inches high, wearing original silk period costume and velvet hair bows, she is considered the national doll of France. If you found one complete with box and label it would be a rare find indeed! Prices of Jumeau dolls vary from $1,000 to $20,000 on the open market.

Bru: France. 1866 to 1899. Master doll maker Bru only made dolls of the highest artistic merit and since almost all his limited production went to aristocracy, they all have fine noble facial features. Strong bodies and very detailed costumes are the telltale characteristics of Bru dolls. Around 1880 he circle-incised his dolls and these all have half-opened mouths, many of which appear to be sucking something like a nipple. Bru dolls, if found, cost in the top range of around $10,000.

J.D. Kestner: Germany. Circa 1880. Small mouths, plump cheeks, spruce faces and German ancestry eyes with subdued expressions identify Kestner dolls. Filled with individualism, Kestner dolls express a taste for life through their eye and mouth expressions. A wide variety of national features are found in Kestner dolls with the oriental models as much in demand as the more traditional European types. Kestner doll prices vary from $1,000 to $10,000.

Godey: France. 1860 to 1916. Known for their sweet beauty and mysterious eyes, Godey dolls had white, almost translucent skin and faintly pink colored cheeks. Some of Godey's dolls were supplied with changes of clothes and as a result were used for

Couch Potato doll. Stuffed, felt, multi-faced, and a whole range of ethnic dolls satisfy any collecting taste.

window ornaments. With expression-filled faces, they were endowed with an almost adult elegance.

Jules Steiner: France. Circa 1880. Jules Nicolas Steiner made terrific mechanical dolls with cute faces that had an almost frightening beauty. Able to fashion dolls that could speak when a screw was turned, they can swing their arms and cry for mommy while exhibiting crying, laughing and sleeping expressions. Using clockwork mechanisms in papier-mâché bodies, Jules Steiner took the art of doll making to a whole new level. Prices of $5,000 to $10,000 are often paid for Steiner dolls in good condition.

Kammer and Reinhardt/Simon & Halbig: Germany. Circa 1890. K&R/Simon & Halbig dolls are distinguished by their open/closed mouth expressions and their detailed embroidery-anglaise dresses. Adorned with exquisitely detailed shoes, boots, bonnets, and pink taffeta 1880s-style gowns, K&R dolls occupy the lower $1,000 to $5,000 bracket of the bisque doll market.

In closing out the golden age of bisque dolls, one must mention the many other fine manufacturers in this crowded, but extremely important toy field. Armand Marseille, Gebruder Haubach, Francois Gaultier and Bruno Schmidt all have a loyal following. And a huge following it is. Antique doll collecting is so popular that it would take many books just to give the reader a detailed picture. Stuffed dolls, felt dolls, multi-faced dolls and a whole range of ethnic dolls satisfy any collecting taste. I would highly recommend dolls for the amateur as it will give you hours of pleasure as well as a handsome profit.

I must also mention the 1930s "Shirley Temple" dolls. These are very collectible and can still be found in the smaller towns of America. Buy any you see. You'll make a great profit, I promise.

Dollhouses

As the antique doll segment grew it spawned subdivisions that have grown up to become collecting divisions of their own. One of these is dollhouses. Furniture accessories, statues, pianos, window decorations and a multitude of hanger-on figurines quickly followed. Since dollhouses are the largest of these subdivisions and often fetch prices as high as the dolls themselves, they warrant a section of their own.

Antique dollhouses manufactured in England and Germany around the mid to late 1800s are most sought after by collectors. Painted and finished with original wallpaper and furniture, "Anne's Pleasure" is a typical example. The house is worth over $5,000 bare, was made in 1860, and has outside walls painted to simulate stone with a sand finish.

Fretted window and door pediments and a slate roof as well as a wood grained front door characterize this dollhouse. The front roof section can be removed to reveal three attic rooms, a sitting room and a bedroom. All rooms are fully furnished with tinplate drawing room furniture, a Regency yew wood table, all curtains, cupboards, and even a Welsh dresser. This, an example of a sought after dollhouse, would go as high as $10,000 at a good auction.

The antique beginner considering dollhouses should bear the following in mind:
1. Condition is essential for high prices.
2. The variety of furnishings included also increases value as does unusual architecture.
3. Dolls' decorations such as shoes and boots in cupboards add character and therefore desirability.

Before I go into teddy bears, the other major item in the antique toy category, I'll quickly fill you in on what the antique toy business calls "automata." Automata antiques are windup, mechanical, musical toys often manufactured in the late 1800s. Dominated by French and German items, they are marvels of mechanical miniaturization. What is interesting about them is the variety available. There's everything from musical rabbits who prick up their ears, to bears with moving jaws who drink liquid from a metal beaker. There's also three bisque headed dolls playing instruments, a nodding peasant figure on a donkey and a walking pig that bellows. These are just a few examples. Difficult to find in good working order, such automata toys fetch anywhere from $700 to $5,000. Keep your eyes open for those made by the French Roullet et Decamps manufacturer, as these are considered the best. An unusual antique category, automata is also highly interesting.

Teddy bears

In 1985 Christie's auctioneers held their first teddy bear and soft toy sale with the expectation that the teddy bear craze would prove short-lived. Much to their surprise they were wrong.

Antique teddy bears are a very large segment in the growing antique toy category. King of the heap are the German Steiff bears followed by the English Deans, Chad Valley and Farnell as well as the American golden plush. Age, quality and condition are all important when collecting teddy bears, but rarity of color and unusual design are also major factors in price determination. Incidentally, the term "Teddy" bear is named after the American President Theodore Roosevelt who held office from 1901 to 1909 and whose story is inexorably connected to the Steiff bear.

Antique teddy bears are a large segment in a growing antique toy category.

In order for the beginner to get a sense of the emotions generated by teddy bears, which cause the subsequent high prices, here is the history of the Steiff bears, now recognized as the top bears to buy.

Steiff: The name Steiff comes from Margerete Steiff, a German girl stricken by polio in the early 1880s. Unable to move and confined to a wheelchair, Margerete Steiff loved visits by neighboring children. She wanted to have something for them to play with, so she made a small toy elephant. Because toys were so rare then, the family was inundated with requests for more. As time went on, Margerete began to train other women to make them in a small factory.

By 1887, Margerete's toys were being sent all over the world and in 1902 her nephew Richard — who spent all his time at the zoo watching bears — made a bear to present to his aunt. Not at all impressed, Margerete nevertheless shipped it to the U.S. Those who saw it laughed at it.

It was returned to Germany the following year, and was displayed at the back of Margerete's booth at the Leipzig Toy Fair. A buyer for a New York import house saw the bear, and immediately ordered 3,000 copies from Margerete's Giengen factory. Before long, he placed another order for 3,000 of the Steiff bears and a legend was born.

Meanwhile, back in America, Theodore Roosevelt's daughter was getting married. Unable to find an appropriate table decoration, the caterer went to New York and saw a Steiff bear in a shop window. Knowing that President Roosevelt was an avid big game hunter, he bought a handful of the bears, decorated them in fishermen and hunter costumes, and placed them on the tables. This delighted everyone at the wedding, including the President. A friend asked Roosevelt, "Say, Teddy, what species are these bears?" to which the President replied: "You've got me there. I think they must be a new species called 'Teddy' bears." When picked up by the press, this little story made the originally rejected Steiff bear famous. Tens of thousands were then ordered from all over the world.

Steiff bears are distinguished by their buttons, earmarks, stitched noses, black button eyes and swiveling head and limbs. They also are more valuable because of the sentimental stories associated with them, which, in turn, leads to higher prices.

Take, for example, Miss Rosa Florella Schmidt. She was the daughter of an English mother and German father and before leaving for Germany in 1914, Rosa's father gave her "Ted," a Steiff bear. Unfortunately Herr Schmidt never returned, apparently killed during the war, and this gift to his daughter became immensely important to her through the years. The bear was all she had to remember her father by and it stayed with her all her life, except for when Rosa evacuated it to the countryside so that it could be safer during the London blitz. Now worth over $8,000, this story adds color to this bear's provenance and increases its value to a collector.

Although Steiff bears are the most valued in this category, many other types make bear collecting both enjoyable and profitable. Many come with nicknames, which increase their value. An amateur should consider only bears in good condition and look for American golden plush types, the English Deans, and bears fitted with growlers.

Recommendation: Amateur collectors should also take an interest in bear accessories like wicker prams. These are becoming increasingly valuable and will develop into a class of their own.

Lead Soldiers and Figurines

Lead soldiers are highly collectible and continue to steadily increase in value. Occupying a specialized section of the toy market, they are not recommended for the amateur unless you have a particular interest in military history. If you do, they will give you endless pleasure. The beginner should consider collecting matching pieces as the value of individual pieces increases with complete sets. Both American and European lead soldiers are popular and priced at between $100 and $500, they are relatively cheap for the amateur investor.

Money Banks

Money banks are highly recommended for the antique amateur. American cast iron "Paddy and the Pig" mechanical banks by J&E Stevens are much sought after but any bank is desirable. Another manufacturer to look out for is the Shepherd Hardware Co. Their 1880 "Stump Speaker" cast iron money bank with patent date on the base is worth close to $10,000, even with some damage.

German made money banks are highly collectible. Most of these are lithographed tinplate made in the early 1900s. Often of wizard, soldier, or sailor characters, German money banks are still a reasonable investment at around $1,000 to $1,500. Saalheimer and Strauss is the manufacturer you should watch out for but this is not as important as good condition and fully working mechanisms.

Money banks are a good investment for the antique beginner.

Tinplate

Tinplate toys cover the whole spectrum of manufacturers — American, German, French, Japanese and English — as well as the whole range of objects. Old cars predominate, but busses, buildings, boats and novelty items are all highly desirable to tinplate collectors. A good investment for the amateur, tinplate toys are relatively plentiful and sure to increase in price as plastic completely replaces tin as a medium of manufacture. Names to watch for are Dinky, Tippco, Schuco Studio, Jouets de Paris, Bing, Richards and Co. and Chad Valley Toys. Many other makers also exist. Condition and the level of interest produced by the toy are the price criteria here which vary from around $200 for a Corgi Batmobile to over $8,000 for a Japanese Nomura mechanized robot called "Robby."

For the amateur interested in tinplate antiques I would recommend that you buy items in first class condition still in original packing. This is not as difficult as it sounds as many of these items were bought by collectors just for this purpose.

A most interesting toy line, tinplate is a wide open category for the amateur. It's reasonably priced and is full of manufacturers who produced a wide variety of interesting products catering to every taste. I particularly like the old tinplate cars with tiny headlamps, red button seats, and hollow rubber tires.

Models

Airplanes, trains, ships and steam engines cover most of the antique model segment. World War I and II fighters are the most sought of the models, but trains are also important. Antique models are reasonably priced, and men are most often the ones

Antique models are reasonably priced.

interested in them. They do not appreciate much in value, however, and therefore are not recommended as an investment for the beginner. Names such as Hornby are familiar to collectors as are the tinplate models of old steam engines by the German manufacturer Doll et Cie. Original packing increases values considerably as does good working condition.

Old galleon sailing ships are used by decorators for pubs and bars and therefore prices are relatively high at around $3,000. Also, be aware that really old and rare 1700 ship models fetch extremely high prices and are considered classics. As an example: An important 1700s British Admiralty dockyard model of a 96-gun Second Rate Ship-of-the-Line fruitwood model with an exposed planked hull and deck, was valued at over $350,000 in 1994. Having said that I should also point out that the gap between such a rare example and the ordinary models found in antique shops is vast, with nothing in between.

Antique models are a specialist's toy item and, while interesting, they are coveted by a very small buying public. Although interesting, models should be invested in for pleasure only.

Miscellaneous Toys

What a huge antique category! Miscellaneous toys cover a whole spectrum of items, some of which fall into their own sections. Here are just a few:

Rocking horses: Antique rocking horses are extremely popular. Parents love them. The plain ones mounted on platforms with wheels or on carved rocking supports are readily available but the rocking horses mounted on metal pivot arms are the cream of the crop. Even if damaged, these are worth buying and repairing. Prices for antique rocking horses vary from $500 for simple ones to $5,000 for the larger, more complex models. They're worth buying as an investment since rocking horses are always in demand and will continue to be so.

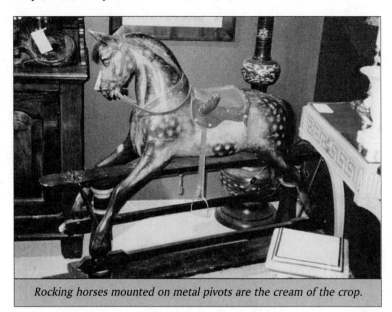

Rocking horses mounted on metal pivots are the cream of the crop.

Pedal cars: A terrific antique toy, metal pedal cars dating from vintage 1903 models to the more modern 1950s examples are always in demand. Some, like the American Gendron Packard twin, are extremely valuable. It's a six-pedal car in original red with black and yellow lining and black wings, wooden chassis, and pressed steel body. A car like this is worth up to $10,000. More affordable models, like the Italian Giordini Indianapolis pedal car in Italian red with cream vinyl upholstery, go for around $2,000. Both are good buys as antique pedal cars in excellent condition have a ready market. Other manufacturers to look out for are Lines Bros., H.J. Mulliner and Triang. My favorite is a yellow 1958 Ferrari Testarossa 250 with welded box section steel chassis, fiberglass body, polished alloy, wood-rimmed steering wheel, working lights and brakes, tonneau cover, clutch-free transmission and pneumatic tires. Worth over $5,000, this is almost like the real thing!

Antique pedal cars are a great investment. Prices will continue to rise.

Disney toys: Papier-mâché Mickey Mouse and Donald Duck displays produced around 1950 are great antique investments. Approximately 26 inches high, these should be snapped up by a beginner if found. The prices will definitely increase above the $700 that was being asked in 1998. Disney toys are a very hot antique collectible, and will probably be as hot as dolls and bears soon.

Noah's Ark playsets: Wooden Noah's Ark playsets as well as wooden Cowboy and Indian Forts are great antique children's toys. Complete sets with animals and Western figurines are valued around $1,500 to $2,500, but intricately carved units depicting biblical or historical events will fetch more. This is a wonderful antique if you have grandchildren. Sometimes called a "Sunday" or "rainy" day antique because it will keep your grandchildren occupied when the weather turns inclement, playsets are also great collectibles.

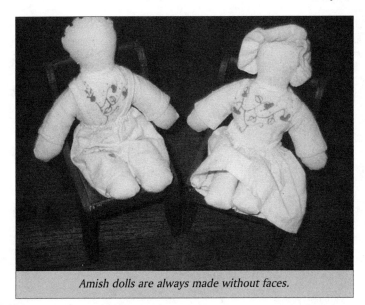

Amish dolls are always made without faces.

Soft Toys: Soft toys, particularly those made in 1920, are gaining popularity. Character figures such as "Bozo the Dog'" are always in demand. The provenance of these toys adds to their value, particularly with ethnic figures made by the European manufacturer Shuco around 1920. Soft toys could be the sleeper in toys with a steadily rising demand.

Antique toys cover a huge selection and many of them have their own corresponding jargon. Here are some common words used by dealers and other experts when showing off.

Pousette: A country, dance figure.

Impressed: When used with dolls it indicates a manufacturer's stamp or marking.

Castellated: Used to describe as having battlements and turrets in dollhouses and wooden playsets.

Lithograph: A print produced by lithography, a printing process in which the image to be printed is rendered onto the metal and treated so that only those areas to be printed will retain ink.

Bebe: French for baby. Remember those old French movies where the hero coos, "Oooh Bebeee!" to the beautiful heroine? Does that date me or what?

Recommendation: Antique toys allow you a lot of freedom as far as choosing what interests you. Dolls and bears are extremely strong and for an antique beginner, I recommend toys strongly.

Here's a story I heard recently: At a garage sale, a friend of mine spied a Shirley Temple doll on a table to one side. She headed quickly in that direction, but was encumbered by the tables of piled up junk. Unfortunately for her, another woman

Antique toys are serious business.

reached the doll first. The gentleman who was watching the sale while his wife was in the bathroom, mistakenly read the price of the doll. "Three-fifty," he said and thanked the woman who gave him three dollars and fifty cents. Needless to say the buyer was out of there before the man's wife returned!

I recommend you find and purchase as many dolls like that as you can.

I also recommend pedal cars. Unlike antique furniture, which should only be tampered with after seeking expert opinion, pedal cars can be repaired to increase their value. Money boxes are another great antique that anyone can tinker with. At prices of around $1,000, they are good value.

Summary

Antique toys are serious business and highly recommended for someone interested in making money from investments in antiques. They can be bought as collector's pieces or for trading. Most categories of toys continue to appreciate with bears and dolls leading the way. Here are some recommendations:

$1,500 and under — Any antique doll, teddy bear or rocking horse.

$1,500 to $5,000 — Any antique doll, teddy bear, rocking horse, or automata.

$5,000 and more — Really old model cars, rocking horses, playsets and any good antique toy with a serious provenance.

Have fun with toys. They are interesting and profitable antique items, as are Islamic, Russian and Tribal antiques — our next category as we get serious again.

Chapter Nine

Tribal, Oriental, Islamic and Russian Antiques

More dealers are opening booths with nothing but tribal art.

The antique business is evolving rapidly. Categories that were previously of little interest to the general public are now becoming part of the mainstream and more and more dealers are opening booths with nothing but tribal art, oriental antiques, or Islamic artifacts. I welcome this. Not only are these new categories extremely interesting and colorful but they are also highly profitable. They do require expert guidance, however, and I would urge an antique beginner to get a valuation from a qualified appraiser before purchasing an expensive tribal, oriental or Russian antique.

Before I give you a brief overview of this increasingly important category I would mention that oriental and Russian antiques are often historical works of art. Knowing the history of the region the item comes from is very important, and nothing beats the public library for gleaning such information. More importantly, be aware that tribal, oriental and Russian antiques have been under sustained attack by unscrupulous fakers in recent years. More so than any other antique category. The reason for this is that with the political changes in the Soviet Union and Africa came a lack of documentation. Many of the fakes are so good that I expect them to become antiques in their own right fifty years hence. Do not, I repeat, do not, buy these antiques from any dealer that isn't reputable and long established. You have been warned!

The growth of tribal antiques is nothing short of phenomenal.

Tribal Art

The growth of tribal art and antiques is nothing short of phenomenal. This has been due to the electronic age making so much more information available to the average dealer. Also, the major auction houses have promoted tribal art more vigorously in recent years.

Most people think of tribal art as mainly African without realizing the extent of what's actually out there. Here are but a few of the various sectors in this promising antique category.

American Indian and Eskimo: The demand for items in this category is fierce, particularly from American collectors. Antique pieces range from very expensive to more modest. A pair of Seminole moccasins sold for $35,000, while items such as Stetsons, buckskin jackets, and chaps from early century "Wild West" shows go for more reasonable and modest sums. Products a beginner should look out for are Indian baskets, tools, utensils, rugs and blankets. Look for things like an 1888 Indian beaded birch bark vase of hexagonal design, with various foliate and geometric motifs in colored beads. Sold for only $900, this will triple in price in five years. Eskimo scrimshaw items and leather work are also much in demand. Old Indian jewelry is another very active sector since genuine antique turquoise and silver is already in short supply.

Indian jewelry is a great reminder as to how antique prices fluctuate. This is illustrated by the following story:

Indian rugs are much sought after, although they must fit the market's unpredictable demands. For example, a 28-by-26 foot Navajo rug called "Little Sister" was knitted in Chilchinbeto, Ariz., and put up for auction at Sotheby's in New York. The tribe expected the rug to sell for about $3.5 million, which they were going to use to fund a clinic. Well, when it was put up for bids, the red, gray and black rug did not produce one, single bid. This, the second of two rugs made on a giant loom built in the 1970s, took ten months to complete. The one made prior was "Big Brother," a 38-by-26 foot world-record sized Navajo rug, that could not be sold due to a prohibitive community ordinance.

Shortly after "Little Sister" was completed, the special loom was destroyed by fire. While "Little Sister" attracted no bidders at the public auction, it did attract a lower private offer.

Ten years from now, I feel the "Little Sister" rug will make the buyer a very rich person. American Indian and Eskimo antiques are exciting. I am split in my view of whether these antiques suit the beginner, especially since genuine pieces are difficult to find and expensive when you do. If you have an interest in Indian folklore I would recommend them. If you're buying for investment purposes only, other tribal antiques may be a better bet due to availability and price. Talking of Eskimo items reminds me of a news item I saw on TV. A woman brought a wooden teardrop shaped bowl to the "Antiques Roadshow" for appraisal. Her husband had stuck it up in the attic where it had been stored until after his death. Imagine her surprise when the appraiser told her it was a rare Eskimo hunting helmet worth over $145,000.

African art and antiques: Accounting for over 50 percent of the tribal antique market, African artifacts are highly sought after by collectors. Recent movies like "Amistad" have only accelerated the demand. Masks, drums, tools, statues, and food containers from the Congo, Gabon, Senegal and Ghana are flying out of antique booths — as long as they are genuine. Yoruba bowls with crusty petinas from Iseyin, Sierra Leone are in demand as are Nomoli soapstone figures and crude Nilotic fibre dolls with an elaborate coiffure of plaited fibre and carved wooden breasts. The Ashanti — one of the most important Ghanaian tribes with a documented history — are a source of terrific items. Pottery lamps modeled in the form of a mother seated on a stool with a child standing between her legs are typical of Ashanti antiques. As are fertility dolls.

The one underlying feature in all African tribal artifacts is that they were principally used to celebrate various festivals. West African tribes, in particular, celebrated a festival virtually every two weeks. Many African antiques are named after festivals such as Egungun, Fao, Apoo and Gologo. The meaning of these depends on where you are but most represent fertility, thankfulness, rain festivals or even sickness festivals.

While on the Ashanti, here is a thumbnail sketch of some of the important tribal groupings whose artifacts are now in demand.

Ashanti: The ancient Ashanti kingdom in Ghana was founded in 1695 when the Ashanti King Asantehene (King) Osei Tutu established Kumasi as its capital. A region rich with gold, lumber and wildlife, the Ashanti are known for their fertility/virility figures which they believe will bless them with prosperity as well as many children. Incidentally, in African tribal custom, children are considered an asset since family structures are paramount.

Yoruba antiques are in demand.

The meaning of these artworks depends on where you are, but most represent fertility, thankfulness, rain forests or even sickness.

Ashanti antiques carved in the early 1900s are most in demand and these can be recognized from their bird motifs.

Recommendation: Fertility dolls, fetish objects, and festival bowls are your best bet. Buy them from reputable importers and dealers as so many fakes exist that it's difficult for anyone to distinguish a genuine piece from a fake.

Yoruba: Also Ghanaian, the western Yoruba tribe celebrates "Shango" (Foremost National Deity) as their premiere god, with others like "Olorun" (The Owner of the Sky) and "Olodumare" (The Almighty) also important. "Obatala," the sculptor god, influences Yoruba artifacts as does "Olorun" who breathes life into bodies. As with the Ashanti, fetishes are a good collector's antique. Incidentally, both these tribes have fetish-priests and the purpose of a fetish is not to harm someone but to protect the owner. Kept for self protection they protect the wearer against sickness, theft, the evil eye and from attacks by wild animals.

Recommendation: Yoruba headdresses such as one for the Egungun masquerade festival, are terrific at prices of around $800. This headdress has a hare carved behind the large ears, a waisted ornament in front, medicine bottles carved on the forehead, and the whole bearded face is painted in bright colors by the Eshubiyi household of Abeokuto. Pairs of carved figurines resembling male and female tribal members are also in demand.

All carvings are good buys.

Makonde: The Makonde tribe of southern Tanzania and northern Mozambique are renowned for their intricate and complicated ebony carvings. Scenes of figures writhing and twisting around each other dominate Makonde carvings, so much so that one has to twist and turn the carving around to figure out where one limb goes and another comes from. Makonde carvings should be snapped up. If found, they fetch high prices on the European markets.

Recommendation: All Makonde carvings are good buys including their folding, three legged stools. Pre-1980 pieces of real ebony are a must. Watch out for fakes blackened with shoe polish to resemble ebony.

Masai: This nomadic tribe from northern Tanzania and southern Kenya is famous for its spears, shields and bird feather headdresses. Renowned for their war-like aggressiveness and nomadic wanderings, the Masai used gourds for storing their main diet mix of blood, milk and urine. These gourds, made from the fruit of the Baobab tree, are always good buys. Incidentally, Africans call the Baobab tree "the upside-down tree" as it looks like it is standing on its head with its branches resembling roots.

As with all African artifacts, the buyer should look for telltale signs that reveal if the items are reproductions. Real antique Masai shields were made from rhino, buffalo or elephant hide and not thin cow hide. The metal tips on spears should have been hand beaten and not poured.

Recommendations: Spears, shields, gourds, knobkerries and headdresses are great buys as long as they are authentic. One of the great things about antiques is that the business of collecting never stands still. Traditional African antiques have always been associated with West African items but these have recently been joined by artifacts from South Africa. Zulu assagais spears, cowhide shields, snuff boxes, headdresses and unusual shaped knobkerries have suddenly experienced unprecedented demand. Early sellers realized profits of over a thousand percent and this trend continues. If you have access to genuine Zulu artifacts, now is the time to buy them. They are highly recommended.

Here is a tip that you will only get in this book:

As demand for Zulu artifacts rises, so will the demand for items from Zimbabwe, Mozambique and Namibia. If you can find old stools, gourds or carvings, buy them. They are bound to appreciate in value, particularly those from around the Zambezi River where the river god Nyaminyami is found on many carvings.

If you can find old stools, gourds, or carvings, buy them.

In closing this brief overview on African artifacts, a word of caution is again in order. Many fakes abound in African tribal art and with prices rising dramatically this is bound to increase. As an antique beginner, if you have a source of supply of genuine artifacts, get them. They will prove to be a great investment.

Polynesian artifacts: Like other ethnic artifacts, Polynesian antiques are appreciating rapidly. A typical example: a Fijian headrest from the Methodist Missionary Society was bought in 1987 for $11,000 and sold recently for $77,000.

The thing that I find interesting about Polynesian artifacts is their wide variety and interesting subject matter. A Samoan bowl for Kava in the form of a turtle has intricately shaped flippers as handles and shell inlay chips for eyes. Worth $6,000, this item came up for sale together with a Solomon Island ceremonial paddle also valued at over $6,000. Real Hawaiian royalty paddles with a provable provenance are known to auction at over $100,000.

Clubs, animal masks, adzes, and even nautilus shell vessels make up the interesting variety in this tribal segment. One item I saw that I particularly liked was a Marquesas Islands smoking pipe. The bowl was carved into a stylized figure, his hands before him flanking an angular panel with geometric motifs. Another supine figure was carved along the length of the stem and the wood had a deep, dark-brown patina caused by many hours of smoking. Worth $5,000, this pipe was both a valuable Polynesian antique and a fascinating piece.

Maori artifacts are in demand. Clubs, staffs, axes and presentation plates are all available on the antique market. With the availability of the Internet, an antique beginner can contact dealers in New Zealand with certifiably genuine antiques if interested in this area of the world. New Guinea is another country from which an increasing number of bird feather headdresses, farming tools, and carved bone artifacts are coming to market. Incidentally, for those readers interested, antiques on the

Internet is now a huge business, which I detailed in my book *More Money From Antiques* available at all bookstores. I would highly recommend it as it covers all aspects of buying and selling antiques in Cyberspace.

For the beginner interested in tribal artifacts I offer a few words of caution. There are two major factors that influence price. The first is that fakes are absolutely flooding the market. With little good provenance available, a scarcity of expert knowledge, and rising prices, a lot of cheap replicas are available. Buy only from long established dealers with references. It is better to pay more than to buy that bargain on which you will probably lose your shirt.

The second problem with tribal antiques is that with so few known and recognized carvers and so many objects that defy classification, tribal art has never been a field for the investor. A relatively small group of enthusiasts pay far too much for items with the unreasonable belief that they may not have another opportunity to obtain such a rare piece again. That is the wrong reason to buy antiques and has ensured that prices continue to rise without the market having an actual basis for doing so. It's like a bubble about to burst. I would hate one of my readers to get caught when it does.

Having offered the above warnings I must also counter by saying that a situation such as this offers profit opportunities for those with nerves of steel to obtain genuine pieces and sell them. Just remember: Don't get greedy. Sell before the whole price structure goes through a correction period, or you will have to wait ages to recoup your costs.

Oriental Antiques

I covered the basics of oriental ceramics in Chapter Two but oriental antiques encompass so much more. As with ceramics, Japanese and Chinese products predominate in this class with objects from the Chinese Ming and Qing Dynasties in the forefront.

Japanese: Besides ceramics, Japanese antiques used brass, silver and bronze as mediums. Often using combinations of such materials, they are beautiful objects d'art. For example, picture a Japanese silver-colored, metal and Shibyama two-handled vase, its body inlaid with mother-of-pearl and polished hard tones on a gold lacquered background with two dragon shaped handles. Its domed quatrefoil base and domed cover decorated with champleve enameled sprays of flowers only adds to the intriguing effect. Sounds exquisite, doesn't it?

Interesting among Japanese bronze antiques are the models of sea life. Crabs, crayfish and swimming carp look terrific and at prices around $500 they are great buys for decorating the fireplace mantel as well as for investment purposes.

Bronze models of Japanese warriors are another underrated Japanese antique. As are bird-life bronzes, such as a late 19th century pair of quails in patinated bronze, colored in copper and gilt, and mounted on a wooden base, all for approximately $3,500.

Recommendation: Japanese bronzes are the sleeper in this terrific category. Netsuke (a small carved or inlaid toggle used to fasten a purse or hold a kimono) is a highly collectible Japanese antique. Mainly made of ivory, or of hardwoods combined with ivory, Netsuke has a collector following. Weird carvings of skulls and distorted faces

Oriental antiques — Japanese and Chinese predominate.

Chinese antiques made from agate, ivory, porcelain, stone, or glass are terrific.

distinguish this interesting class of collectibles, which are difficult to find for under $500. If you stumble over a genuine ivory Netsuke, I would recommend you buy it. There is a ready market for them.

Trays, teapots and vases or jardinieres, all highly decorated with inlays or enamels of foliage, pagodas, or flowers, form the bulk of desirable Japanese antiques. All are a good bet for the beginner, in particular the bronzes, and I recommend buying them as an investment, or purely for pleasure.

Chinese: Snuff bottles, snuff bottles, and more snuff bottles! Wonderful antiques, Chinese snuff bottles made from agate, ivory, porcelain, stone, or glass are terrific antique buys. Priced under $1,000, they are much in demand and will continue to be so.

Chinese snuff bottles are beautifully carved, come adorned with Zodiac signs, figurines, bamboo, and flower patterns, and are all intricately inlaid with mother-of-pearl and gilt metals. If you find them, buy them!

Oriental antiques are good products for the amateur. Get yourself a good book on periods and markings and you can't go wrong with Chinese and Japanese items, particularly collector pieces like Netsuke or Chinese snuff bottles.

A 1920 Persian "Serapi" valued at $10,000 to $12,000.

Islamic Artifacts

Islamic artifacts have a growing following, particularly in Europe. The trend is bound to catch on in the U.S. and one can already find Islamic antique stores in the major cities like New York and Los Angeles.

Islamic antiques have a very distinctive style and come mainly from the Middle East and North Africa. Personally, I like them. Highly decorative, bright in color and dating back to the Coptic 5th and 8th century A.D., they offer interesting insight into history. They also require an expert dealer to identify pieces and as such are too difficult for an antique beginner to buy and sell unless one is prepared to do a lot of research.

Just to complicate matters further, Islamic antiques date back to many periods, from Constantine the Great (307 to 337 A.D.) to the Byzantine period, the Ottoman Empire, the Roman Empire and the Mamluk periods, to name just a few. Unlike English antiques, which fall into distinct periods easily identified by Kings' or Queens' reigns, Islamic items have no such clear distinctions.

Having sounded cautionary, I do, however, see opportunities in Islamic antiques for a beginner willing to put a lot of time into studying and research. Islamic antiques are still reasonably priced and will appreciate substantially over the next few years.

Here is a selection of items that I would recommend.

1. 13th to15th century Persian pierced bronze bowls, vases and trays.
2. Tribal silver jewelry from Saudi Arabia, Yemen, Oman and Afghanistan. Antique hookah smoking pipes and old inlaid brass coffeepots together with their braziers and cups.
3. Ottoman mother-of-pearl veneered boxes inlaid with ivory. These are wonderful works of art and often come with silver, bone and hardwood banding. They are often lined with silk or velvet.
4. Turkish brass candlesticks. Many from the 17th century have faceted stems above tulip-shaped bosses and flared, serrated rims.
5. Ottoman enameled copper jars with gold scrolling in the form of leafy vine motifs.

Also Persian, Kurdish or Turkoman rugs.

When I think of rugs, it reminds me how popular Persian carpets have recently become. Many people still don't realize that real antique rugs are over 100 years old and were entirely made by hand in an area stretching from Istanbul in the west to Sinkiang, China, in the east. The oldest producing countries or regions were Anatolia (now Turkey), the Caucasus (southern area of the old Soviet Union), Persia (now Iran), Afghanistan, Central Asia (Turkmenistan, Uzbekistan, Kirgizstan) and Tibet/Nepal.

Hand woven, oriental carpets were often made from start to finish by just a handful of related people who shaved the wool from the family or village sheep, dyed it in vats filled by an expert dye master, and wove it on family looms. Hence their price.

Islamic artifacts and antiques are extremely interesting but require an expert's eye and knowledge. If you are prepared to learn everything about them then they are definitely worth investing in as prices are still reasonable. Me, I personally like Islamic artifacts.

Recommendation: Stick to hookah pipes, intricate vases, and smaller Persian rugs as a collector. That way you can't make too many mistakes while gaining the necessary knowledge to collect more valuable pieces.

Russian Antiques

Who hasn't heard about Faberge and their fabulous eggs? Or the Tsarist treasure from the Imperial Romanov period? Russian antiques were all the rage a few years ago, icons in particular. It was almost as if all the icons were being sucked out of Russia, and you could find very valuable pieces anywhere — even at antique fairs. Not anymore. Not only has the Russian

Who hasn't heard about Faberge and their fabulous eggs?

Russian antiques were all the rage a few years ago.

government belatedly stopped exports of antiques without complicated documentation, but the Russian people have realized how valuable their possessions are. Organized crime has come into the picture, and Russian antiques are now very difficult to obtain. If you can, buy items that are not as glamorous as icons, but certainly as valuable and useful.

Russian glass: Russian cut and engraved glass is terrific value. Russian glass factory goblets and bowls engraved with a profile portrait of Czarina Elizabeth Petrovna can still to be found for around $1,000. Wine glasses decorated with crowned shield medallions not only look extremely elegant but are good value at $1,000 a pair. An amateur should always look out for Russian glass engraved with portraits of famous people as these are where resale demand lies.

Eggs: Both porcelain and pottery eggs are much in demand. Mainly painted with religious scenes, such as Christ holding the cross, and often gilded with gilt or gold, Russian eggs are really good antiques. If you can find Russian eggs in great condition and it must be great then buy them. Demand for hand-painted Russian eggs continues to grow.

Faberge: One can't mention eggs without Faberge springing to mind. Unfortunately most of us will never be able to afford these wonderful antiques, but Faberge also manufactured imperial presentation trophies, photograph frames, enameled desk clocks, bell-pushes, compacts, decanters, brooches and kovshes. All these appreciate in value and are worth collecting.

Russian silver: Russian silver antiques are valuable, particularly those manufactured in the late 1800s. Items such as silver cigar boxes engraved and chased overall to simulate cigar brands, composite silver toilette sets by Efim Siderov, St. Petersburg, and snuff boxes, presentation pieces, pictorial jewelry boxes, tea sets, cups and saucers and sets of spoons in original fitted boxes are wonderful antiques. Look for pieces from famous Russian names such as P. Ovchinnikov, F. Ruckert, I. Khlebnikov, O. Kurluvukov, Sazikov and M. Semenova. The kovshes of various sizes are much in demand. Best bet: silver vodka cups.

Porcelain: Russian antique porcelain is second to none in quality. The imperial porcelain factory made excellent military and pictorial plates, vases, and Easter cipher eggs. The 1830 Nicholas I vases are much sought after and dining sets are also in demand. Complete sets from the Kornilov Factory and vases from the Gardner and Batenin factory are easily recognizable due to their detail, and are much desired.

Icons: The demand for genuine Russian icons is huge! The icons produced from the 15th century through the early 20th century period are snapped up quickly and many cover a multitude of religious subjects. Icons encased in ornate silver oklads with silver filigree, pearls, and gems are the ones everyone wants if you can find them or afford them.

Exotic antiques are fun. Extremely colorful, these require expert knowledge.

Russian bronzes and watercolors: Watercolor paintings, like all artworks based on an artist's reputation, require expertise. As do bronzes. The Russian artists who have a reputation in this segment are Makovsky, Bogdanov-Belsky, Orlov, Grachev and Dobuzinsky.

Imperial antiques: Experts in Russian antiquities group a number of items in the category of imperial antiques including porcelain eggs with cyphers, photographs of the imperial family, bronze statues of Nicholas II and coronation volumes, documents, and letters.

There are a wide range of exotic antiques, which makes them quite fun. They're extremely colorful and require expert knowledge if you are going to be skilled enough to avoid the many fakes. If you invest intelligently, these can be highly profitable.

Here are some of the colorful words used when discussing tribal, oriental, Islamic and Russian antiques.

Sierra Leone: A diamond-rich country on the west coast of Africa. It was one of the last stops on the slave trade route and has a turbulent history.

Kava: An intoxicating beverage made from the root of an Australasian Kava plant.

Cassowary feathers: Feathers from a large flightless bird found in New Guinea and adjacent areas. It has a bony projection on the top of the head and brightly colored wattles.

Arabesque: An intricate and ornate design of intertwined floral, foliate, and geometric figures.

Repousse: Shaped or decorated with patterns in relief made by hammering and pressing on the reverse side.

Knop: A decorative knob.

Jardiniere: A large, decorative vessel for displaying flowers.

Mamluk: A member of a military caste composed of slaves from Turkey that held the Egyptian throne from 1250 until 1517 and remained powerful until 1811.

Recommendation: A beginner wishing to get involved in foreign antiques would well be advised to stick to the easily identifiable items.

> $1,500 and under — I recommend the Japanese Netsuke, Chinese snuff bottles, and goblets by the Russian Imperial Glass factory.

> $1,500 to $5,000 — I recommend Russian silver cigarette and cigar boxes, small Persian rugs, and Ashanti headdresses.

> $5,000 and more — This class is so full of great antiques costing above the five-thousand dollar mark that it's difficult to make suggestions, but I think that imperial porcelain eggs with cyphers, tribal silver jewelry from Saudi Arabia, and Polynesian or New Guinea headdresses, canoe paddles, and royal utensils will appreciate. Old American native Indian artifacts are also without doubt excellent investment items.

Summary

An incredibly varied class of antiques, oriental, Islamic and American native antiques are a rapidly growing segment. African tribal antiques suffer from too many fakes as do Russian artifacts. For that reason only, they are best avoided.

Before moving back into the more normal antique sector of clocks, watches, barometers and grandfather longcase clocks, I would like to reiterate that the above classes of antiques are highly interesting and that if you, as an amateur, are prepared to put in the time to learn them inside out, they can be extremely profitable.

Time to move on and discuss longcase clocks and other things that go tick in the night.

Chapter Ten

Clocks, Barometers and Instruments

Antique clocks take us back to French, German, Swiss, English, and Italian manufacturers.

Clocks, barometers, and scientific instruments are wonderful antiques and extremely popular, especially with men. There's something about people that makes them want to tinker with intricately tuned mechanical clockwork functions. Many turn it into a new business once they retire and find themselves working even harder than they did during their careers, often for a terrific profit.

Antique clocks take us back to French, German, Swiss, English and Italian manufacturers, all of whom made clocks and watches in clearly defined periods. We shall also cover American clock manufacture, which has its own famous makers. Being the craftsmen they were, clock makers made various types of timepieces ranging from stand-alone longcases (grandfather clocks) to pocket watches. To make antique timepieces understandable to the amateur, I shall cover each category separately. Since terminology is important in discussing antique clocks, I shall define terms as we go. Incidentally, an antique clock and watch repairer is officially called an "antiquarian horologist," and in both the U.S. and England they have very influential associations. Before going into the different types of antique clocks, a brief history lesson is in order.

When was the first clock made?

No one is sure, but sundials can be classified as the earliest clocks recorded in history. There were also candle clocks that measured time by burning candles and water clocks that did the same by dripping water. These were called "clepsydras," or water-clocks, and though they were fairly widespread in their time, only a few examples still exist today, in England.

The first recorded sketch of a mechanical escapement (the part of the clock that stops and releases the gear movements at measured intervals) comes from circa 1250. The first recorded references to iron clocks were made in the 14th century when, in 1364, Italian Giovani da Dondi described a mechanical clock movement. The oldest known mechanical clock dates back to 1389, and can be found in Rouen, France.

As far as we (antique clock collectors) are concerned, the most important date is 1657 when Dutchman Christian Huygens invented the pendulum escapement. Incidentally, here is a quirky question with a quirky answer.

Q: Why is the Roman numeral IV written IIII on clock dials?

A: Although IIII is a valid way of writing Roman numerals, it was traditionally used by clock makers for aesthetic balance. If it were written as IV, you would have IV and V on the lower right side and VII and VIII on the lower left making the clock face look lopsided, as if it wanted to roll to the left. Just to be eccentric, as many Englishmen are, London's Big Ben uses IV rather than IIII to maintain balance.

That's enough history. Here are the various types of antique clocks on the market together with their characteristics. Not all the terms used are familiar in the U.S., but since they are known in Europe I shall use them.

An English shelf clock.

Bracket clocks: The dictionary defines "bracket" as a small shelf supported by brackets, among other things. Bracket clocks are therefore small shelf clocks and fall into a size from 15 to 24 inches. All are spring driven, most "bracketed" in a square case with corner pillars and feet, and have decorative tops with or without a handle. Almost all are eight-day clocks meaning that their spring, when wound, takes eight days to totally uncoil. They often come with Roman numerals for the hour indications and range from simple units, like a walnut-cased one by Garrards that has Westminster chimes, silver chapter ring dial and gilt metal mask spandrels, and sells for about $500, to the more complex John Jackson of Portsea, England, Victorian model with ebonized case, triple-train fusee movement with eight bells and gong at a price of about $4,000.

From these descriptions you can see that clock "lingo" is an art in itself. This should not discourage an amateur from trading in antique clocks, which are a major category in the antique business. There are, however, so many manufacturers and technical features that govern clock prices that I recommend you buy a specialized book detailing these. It's advisable for you to carry it around with you for reference. There are too many details to remember otherwise.

Bracket clocks made in England and Europe are often referred to by their period of manufacture, namely Victorian, Regency, Louis XV, etc., as well as by their manufacturer. This is standard procedure with all types of European clocks, although American clock makers used their names as distinguishing references.

Here are some American and European clock manufacturers whose names guarantee a good antique clock investment.

American: The Ansonia Clock Co., 1850-1929; Westerbury Clock Co. 1857-1944; Seth Thomas, 1813-1853; Various Seth Thomas Clock Co.'s, 1853-1930 (antiques); Gilbert Manufacturing, 1866-1871; Ingraham & Co., 1857-1958; and F. Kroeber, 1863-1904.

English: Thomas W. Field, James Chater, London; A. Irving, London; James (Jas) McCabe, Royal Exchange London; William Johnson Stock Exchange, London; and W. Tomlinson, London. As mentioned previously, English clocks are also described as Georgian, Victorian, and Regency if made in the dates I detailed in Chapter Two on furniture.

French: Balthasard, Paris; Japy Freres, Paris; Perache a Paris, Le Sieur a Paris, Achille Brocot, Paris; Raingo Freres, Paris; Cotonie, Paris; and Guyerdet & Bouilly a Paris.

German/Austrian: Adolf Hradetzkn; Brunn; Grande Sonnerie; Kriedel Cs. Both; Gustaf Becher and C.J. Klaftenberger.

Italian: Ganzinotto, Genoa.

Carriage clocks: Carriage clocks are antique traveling clocks with brass or silver cases and are distinguishable by their 4-1/2 to 6 inch size and their top carrying handles. Used on journeys, they were often hung on a special hook next to the lantern on the horse and buggy carriages. Almost all antique carriage clocks are eight-day spring clocks and some came with leather traveling cases to protect them.

All carriage clocks have gong or bell alarms and the early 1900s ones have an alarm dial at the bottom. Many of the better makes strike both the hour and the half hour and most have simple stark white enameled dials for ease of visibility in candlelight. Aren't antiques wonderful? Most people don't really know why carriage clocks came with white enameled faces but now that you do you can slip it into a conversation and baffle a dealer who considers himself an expert.

Tip: When buying carriage clocks, or any clock for that matter, make sure that you get the wind-up key with it. They are very difficult to find.

At prices ranging from $500 to $5,000, carriage clocks are great antiques for the beginner. Make sure they work before shelling out your money, though! Repairing antique clocks is an expensive business and small carriage clocks with minute working parts will cost you even more to repair.

Garnitures: The word garniture means an embellishment and when used with antique clocks means a clock flanked by two glasses, vases, or candleholders made to the same design. Used to decorate mantelpieces, a three-piece garniture is a pretty ensemble. Mainly French, these three-piece sets were made by Boulle and T. Simpson et Cie, Paris. Priced at between $2,000 and $5,000, they are in reasonable demand. If considering buying garnitures, an amateur antiquer should make sure that the accessories are in top condition and aren't chipped. Too many beginners think that if the clock is fine then the pair of candlesticks need not be as good. This is a mistake. Price depends on condition of all three pieces.

Lantern clocks: Lantern clocks are the creme de la creme of small mantel or table clocks and are very much in demand. They're reaching prices of upwards of $10,000 for a George II lantern timepiece with alarm signed by John Belling Bodmyn 1753. Lantern clocks are very distinguishable. Made entirely of metal with a visible bell at the top, they date back to the 1700s and are marvels of miniaturization. Virtually all solid brass, approximately 6 to 8 inches high, they have bold brass faces with distinctive hour and minute hands. Made in England, lantern clocks were shipped all over the world and with pierced brass decorations and prominent bell domes to chime the hours, they cannot be mistaken.

It's worth mentioning at this stage that many European makers did not produce their own mechanical works but bought various working parts and then assembled them. This does not detract from the clock's value as many makers modified the works to suit their own particular requirements.

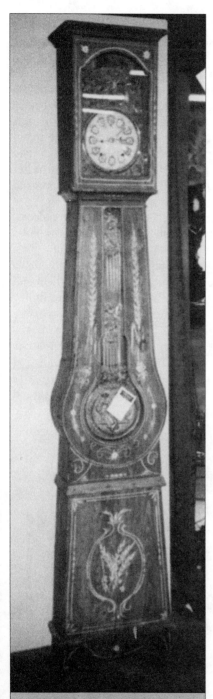

Longcase clocks allowed makers full reign to practice their artistic carpentry.

Almost all longcase clocks are eight-day or pendulum timepieces.

Longcase clocks: Antique longcase clocks allowed manufacturers free reign to practice their artistic carpentry and most of the clock cases are truly works of art. Using rain forest mahogany, burr walnut, and other exotic woods, they produced clocks with marquetry, checker board inlay, and japanned finishes. (Japanned means it was varnished and decorated in black enamel or lacquer finish in the Japanese manner.) Being large artistic pieces, longcase clocks quickly became symbols of wealth and every substantial household in the English 1700s and 1800s had to have one prominently displayed in the entry hall. Because the competition was fierce among people trying to find those with recognized "names," longcase craftsmen became specialized and prospered. Names like Richard Corless from Stockport, G.H. Bell from Winchester and Ben Kimberly, Catskill, were in demand and their longcase clocks command good prices.

Almost all longcase clocks are eight-day weight driven or pendulum timepieces. Many have four- or five-pillar movements with striking bells and the brass clock faces are always adorned with regal looking Roman numerals and silver rings.

In recent years, longcase clock prices have remained stagnant. This may be due to modern homes no longer having entry halls large enough to accommodate them and the fact that longcase clocks are difficult to move around. When they are moved they often require expert resetting and this is not a cheap expenditure. Prices for name brand antique longcases start around $2,000 and reach $20,000 for really rare ones.

I would not recommend longcase clocks to an amateur antiquer for the reasons mentioned above. Modern antique buyers like to carry their merchandise home and you would be better off investing in bracket, lantern, or mantel clocks. Check longcases out, however, as they are beautifully made and are fine examples of Georgian and Queen Ann carpentry.

A decorative mantel. A great piece of furniture as well as a place for a mantel clock.

Mantel clocks: Mantel clocks average 13 to 24 inches in size and apart from telling the time, act as decorative centerpieces on the mantel shelf. Most are very elaborate, particularly the popular French ormolu ones. The American Ansonia Watch Co. followed French design trends and Ansonia mantel clocks are sought after by American collectors. A 16-inch high, four-glass sided Ansonia with cream stepped dial, exposed Brocot gong striking movement, and cast case with leafy scrolls and floral clusters sells for around $1,500. If you find one of these in a flea market, buy it.

Mantel clock manufacturers used their imaginations to the fullest. Gold, ornate clocks with floral decoration, harp shaped clocks, clocks with top mounted figurines, carved, walnut clocks with scenes of deer climbing a rocky mound and even a "Chariot of Diomedes" clock with the wheel as the dial are to be found. The variety is endless and mantel clocks rack up big sales for antique dealers. More a decorative piece than a clock, mantel clocks are an obvious living room status symbol.

French, Austrian and English clocks dominate the mantel clocks segment with American Ansonia products mixed in. Unlike other clocks, design and style are the popular criteria and other than Louis Phillipe, no major names stand out. The 18th and 19th century periods are the ones to buy with pretty lady scenes painted in enamel as first choice.

Prices for mantel clocks vary from $800 to $8,000. A great antique segment for the amateur, mantel clocks have a wide market and supply is reasonable.

Skeleton clocks: Rare but very attractive, skeleton clocks make interesting conversation pieces. They're made of brass, and are fascinating to watch. Because of their rarity, prices for good working models vary from $1,500 to $10,000.

Most skeleton clocks I have seen were Victorian period English-made ones. Popular names to look for are J.D. Taylor of Liverpool, Parker and Pace of Bury St. Edmonds, and Alfred Smith of Huddersfield. **Recommendation:** Skeleton clocks are good antiques for the beginner if you can find them. Because they're so rare they are profitable collector's pieces. Besides that, who can resist all the visible intricate wheels, balances, levers and springs?

Wall clocks: Much in demand, antique wall clocks find a ready market. As with mantel clocks, style and decorative design are more important than manufacturer. Also of interest, wall clocks come in picture design silvered metal, porcelain Black Forest design and in rather stern mahogany inlay. All have easily readable dials and pointers. German

Much in demand, antique wall clocks find a ready market.

manufacturers and their pretty wooden cuckoo clocks are well known but difficult to find. English-made 1800 wood-cased pendulum clocks, however, are easily available. The French concentrated on manufacturing wall clocks in metal and open-faced porcelain and these have their own substantial following.

Prices for wall clocks range from $1,000 to $8,000. Another good line for the antique beginner because of the variety on the market, wall clocks sell well.

Summary: Clocks offer the antiquer a great opportunity. Supply is sufficient, the variety extensive, and the demand constant. More a household decoration then an essential timepiece, clocks — particularly skeleton and lantern clocks — are extremely interesting items to behold.

Tips: Make sure the clock is in working order. While repairing them is no problem with thousands of part-time antiquarian horologists around, it is fairly expensive. Condition is also paramount. Used as decorative pieces, damaged clocks are difficult to sell. Tastes also dictate popularity. In southern states the intricate ormolu French models are the No. 1 seller while the mahogany cased pendulum clocks sell better in northern states like Michigan and New York.

Recommendation: Antique mantel and wall clocks are a must for the amateur. While the innards are difficult to figure out with all sorts of movements complicating matters, they are not as important as good working order and excellent exterior condition.

Closing out clocks, I am now going to tell you a story before moving on to watches.

A man was sitting in a Scottish pub steadily getting drunk. He had popped in before going to the store to look for a birthday present for his wife. "One wee dram won't do me any harm," he had convinced himself four hours earlier.

Thrown out at closing time the cold air revived him and he remembered the birthday present. "Ooooh me gosh," he mumbled, "Oi'm in deep cow doo now. Te woife will kill me if I don' bring her sum'mit home!"

Just then he spied an antique store closing up across the street. Without hesitation he ran in. In no condition to look around, he decided to buy his wife the longcase grandfather clock just inside the door. "Me ol' lady's always wanted one of t'ose," he mumbled.

"We can deliver it tomorrow," the pleased antique dealer said, huffing and puffing with impatience to close the door. Now that he had the money he wanted to go home.

"Oooh, nooo. Te ol' lady will kill me, she will. Oi'll carry it home, meself," the drunk said and helping him lift it onto his back the antique store owner sent him on his way, stumbling and weaving across the road.

As the drunk crossed the last alley before his house the clock was getting to be too heavy to hold. Swaying from side to side he was bumped by a late night jogger, out exercising.

Getting up as best he could the drunk looked at the concerned jogger with bleary eyes and asked rudely: "Oi! Why do'n you look where you are going, yee ken?"

The jogger looked at him for a moment, turned his head slightly to avoid the whiskey fumes and snapped back: "Why don't you wear a wristwatch like everyone else, yee ken?"

Watches: Rare, not so rare, expensive and not so expensive — antique watches come either as fob (pocket) watches, also called hunter watches, or as wristwatches. They are definitely gentlemen's timepieces and were associated with landed gentry and business tycoons. In the days of parasols, top hats and horse and buggy carriages, no gentleman would be caught dead without his waistcoat and his pocket watch, replete with gold chain. Held in high esteem, they were given to loyal workers retiring from a lifetime of service with the same company. Oh well, times have changed, haven't they? Now all we get is a pink slip!

Pocket watches by Waltham, USA, Phillipe Patek, Geneva and J.W. Benson, Ludgate Hill, London, are coveted by antique collectors. Other popular makers were Fresard Watch Co., Lucerne Switzerland, the 19th century New Haven Watch Co., Movado Watch Co., Piguet & Co. and the 1847 creations by Thomas Earnshaw of London.

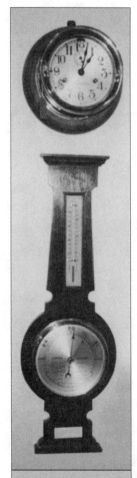

Many 18th century pocket watches are of gold or silver and are beautifully and decoratively engraved. They are real works of art with many hours of loving skill put into the designs. Prices on the antique market for silver pocket watches vary from $200 to $1,000 and those made of gold from $1,000 to $10,000. Some nickel ones were made by Waltham in the U.S. and can be found for less than $200.

Quaint looking with their windup knobs on the top, pocket watches are a side player in the antiques business and collected by enthusiasts only. An interesting clothing accessory, they are not recommended for the beginner interested in the commercial end of the antique business. Not enough demand exists among the general public. Like waistcoats, fob watches are part of a bygone era.

Wristwatches: Who does not covet a $50,000 gold Rolex?

Antique wristwatches are big business! Not only are they lusted after by antique collectors worldwide whose penchant for paying increasingly higher prices seems never ending, but they are also the status symbol "de riguer" for the nouveau riche.

The antique wristwatch business is dominated by precision-made Swiss products. Gruen, Rolex, Cartier, Patek Phillipe and Gallet are all at the top of this hectic antique segment. Gold predominates as the metal of choice and rare, unusually designed antique wristwatches fetch astronomical prices. For example: A rare and unusual 1928 cushion calendar watch by Patek Phillipe went for close to $400,000 at auction in 1993. What it would fetch today is anybody's guess, but I would not hesitate to say one million.

Recommendation: You only have to check the advertisements in major newspapers to realize how big a business antique watches are. Half page advertisements offering expensive oyster Rolex's are placed weekly, often accompanied by

Antique barometers are popular home decoration items.

Stick barometers suffer from the fact that bulbs and tubes are exposed and get broken.

enticing offers to buy any Rolex available. I like antique watches. If you do, too, I would recommend you start at the low end of the scale and work your way up. You never know, you might find an old Rolex on some Idaho potato farmer's wrist and he might just take $1,000 cash for it. If you do and don't want it, just call me!

Closing out this segment on clocks and watches, I had a feeling of bemusement come over me. Looking at the beautiful gold pocket watches available and comparing them to the $400,000 Patek Phillipe calendar watch made me think of how unfair life is. Not that there's anything wrong with the calendar watch. It's just that the ornate enamel and gold fob watches are so much more beautiful. Not only that, most of them represent a lifetime of someone's hard work, yet sell for only around $200.

The more I think about it the more I feel that pocket watches might be the up-and-coming thing, even though I expressed my doubts earlier in this chapter. I think I'll go out and purchase a few at low prices before the nouveau riche discover them. Isn't that what the antique business is all about anyway? Taking a gamble and possibly making a fortune because you are one step ahead of the crowd?

Barometers

Antique barometers are popular home decoration items and can be found in most antique auctions. The normal ones are the wheel shaped aneroid barometers with circular pressure dials and long strip thermometers with a bottom bulb. Averaging from $150 to $3,000, these enjoy a steady demand. For the beginner I would recommend that you stick to the mahogany cased ones, many of which date back to the 1700s. The more carved the wood the easier they are to sell. Just make sure that the glass cover is not crazed or yellowed as, once again, condition is important.

Stick barometers in good condition are rare, and the very fact that the bulb and tube are exposed is their downfall. Although normally valued at approximately $2,000, there was one that sold at a manor auction house for $80,000. It was a rare 1725 George I walnut barometer by J. Halifax of Barnsley, England, with mask spandrels, finely engraved scrolling leaves, and was set with an engraved recording dial. You just can never tell.

Plain round wheel barometers, Dutch inlaid walnut barometers with pewter plates, marine barometers with ivory dials, and original brass cistern and gimbals English walnut pillar barometer with finials controlling the pointers fill this class. George III mahogany and boxwood barometers round out this category. A good sideline, barometers make an excellent match to antique wall clocks.

Antique globes have the biggest share of the scientific instrument market.

Scientific Instruments

Scientific instruments are mainly men's antiques. Sought after by professionals and occasionally by interior decorators they are not a generally traded antique except among avid collectors. They do, however, cover sections such as world globes, which have a broader market. Here is a brief list.

Globes: Antique globes have the biggest share of the scientific instrument market because they make a terrific decorative piece for the study or den. They are not cheap and the large celestial ones set into mahogany frames cost as much as $5,000.

What is wonderful about globes is that they are often mounted in brass meridian and horizontal rings and have fascinating legends inscribed on them. The 1880 period English globes made by Blades, East and Blades, London, and by Edward Stanford of Charing Cross, London, are in demand. If you find an old globe with the name of the maker inscribed or printed somewhere I would suggest you buy it. They always appreciate and sell quickly. Globes are definitely a "nouveau riche" home furnishing item.

Telescopes: Antique telescopes have a strong following of enthusiasts. With the recent asteroid movies and interest in astrology on the rise this should continue in the future. Brass refracting telescopes also make highly decorative additions to furnishings in elegant homes. Prices vary but name brand ones can be bought in higher-end antique malls for $800 to $5,000. English names such as R&J Beck, London; James Short, London; and Newton and Sons, Opticians, London, are known and desired by enthusiasts. A good item for the antiquer if found in first class condition, telescopes are fun.

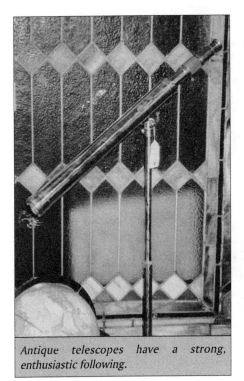

Antique telescopes have a strong, enthusiastic following.

Surveying instruments: Brass quadrants, sextants, theodolites and drawing instruments complete this antique segment. Of these, marine sextants are the most popular due to the number of "old sea dogs" that harbor nostalgic feelings for their good old seafaring days. Good antique sextants sell for around $1,000 to $2,000 and usually come complete with case. As with antique telescopes and globes, most of these are of English manufacture by named companies such as Harris and Son, London; Andrew Yeates, London; and J. King and Son, Bristol, which are all 18th and 19th century seaports.

Antique sextants are fun instruments and sell well.

Microscopes and medical instruments: Purchased mainly by doctors to decorate their offices, antique microscopes and surgeon's instruments are in short supply. They are a good buy for this reason and for the fact that those in the medical profession have more disposable income than most to buy them. If you can find such instruments in good condition, you will always find a buyer by advertising in the medical section of your local paper.

As someone who hates being sick, I find antique surgeon's tools really strange. Many of them look almost like torture instruments. One item I saw in researching this book was a leather and iron surgical corset circa WW I. Just thinking of putting it on made me shudder. It looked like a tin body coffin! Some of the metal ear trumpets weren't much better. How patients could stand the cold metal tube being stuck down their ear, I don't know. An English, carved ivory phrenology head with yellow patina worth over $4,000 also made me chuckle. Having lived in Africa much of my life I could only wonder what the elephant whose tusks were used to make this schematic human head would have thought.

A long chapter but an interesting one. Here are some reference words that get thrown about.

Ormolu: Gold imitation.

Fob: A small pocket at the front of a waistcoat or a short chain attached to a pocket watch.

Phrenology: The study of the conformation of a skull based on the belief that it is indicative of mental ability or character.

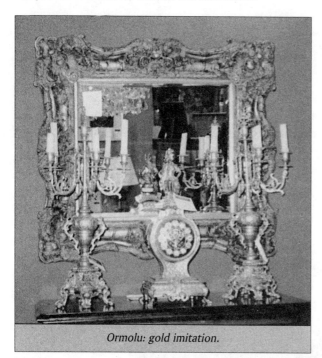

Ormolu: gold imitation.

Frets: An ornamental design composed of repeated and symmetric figures, often in relief, contained within a band or border.

Spandrels: The space between two arches and a horizontal cornice.

Pilasters: A supporting column or pillar.

Lunette: A small, crescent-shaped space.

So many products spring to mind that it is difficult to decide what to recommend.

Fusee movement: A grooved cone-shaped pulley movement used to equalize the mainspring's force by maintaining a differential winding and unwinding of the cord or chain from the spring container.

Thermometer box: A graduated glass tube with mercury that rises with temperature.

Equinoctial: Relating to an equinox.

Theodolite: A surveying instrument for measuring horizontal and vertical angles.

Refracting: Deflecting light from a straight path.

Lignum Vitae eyepiece: A wooden eyepiece made from the tropical Lignum Vitae tree.

Monaural stethoscope: A stethoscope recording or reproducing sound channeled into a single carrier.

Fun, weren't they? Strange too!

Recommendation: So many products spring to mind in this category that it is difficult to decide what to recommend.

> $1,500 and under — Mantel clocks and carriage clocks must be the first choice. George III longcase clocks are also a good bet.

> $1,500 to $5,000 — Wristwatches, fob watches, and globes are definitely the desirable antiques at these prices and complicated carriage clocks with calendar work or striking arrangements also fit in at this price.

> $5,000 and above — It's the expensive wristwatches that take the class, since demand for these seems insatiable. Mind you, today's news says that Japan is in deep recession and this might cool such demand down.

Summary

This has been a huge category with lots of fascinating product lines. A beginner should stick to the ones with wide market appeal, but so many antiques carry such interesting histories that in the end it will depend on your own preference.

That was interesting. Let's move on, shall we?

A beautiful wooden mantel clock.

Chapter Eleven

Militaria

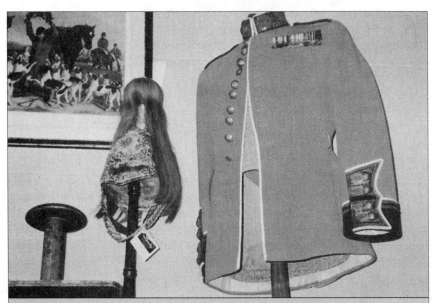

Military antiques, so long the preserve of nostalgic old men reliving war stories, is big business.

On one of the many TV antique shows, a woman in Massachusetts brought in what looked like a conical shaped piece of beaten tin. She had found it jammed in the rafters of an old barn on some property she had recently bought and, curious about its origin, she cleaned it before requesting a free valuation.

As is usual on these shows, the appraiser, who was virtually bug-eyed, asked her a lot of lead-in questions before rapidly blurting out that what she had found was a circa 1600 cabasset (helmet) worth at least $250,000 at auction. As you can imagine, the lady nearly fell off her chair.

Military antiques, the preserve of nostalgic old men reliving war stories, are big business.

Pistols, rifles, armor, swords and a whole host of military items now crowd this field which, while still the preserve of men, is fast gaining an audience of appreciative women dealers. I have even heard of one woman who concentrates on antique memorabilia connected to women's roles in warfare throughout the ages. And why not? Although nursing was their initial forte, women in the military go back as far as "Bodecia the Chariot Queen," and women's exploits as drivers, spies, mechanics and pilots are now gaining recognition. Who hasn't heard of Florence Nightingale and Odette the French spy?

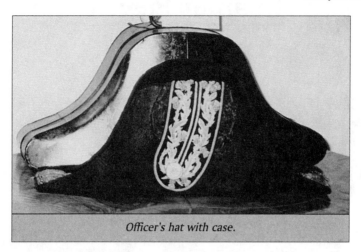
Officer's hat with case.

For the antique beginner, militaria does pose problems. Detailed knowledge is required in the field as the specialist market is the main sales outlet. This is one of the factors that makes militaria a harder-than-normal antique segment to enter unless you are extremely interested in it. As illustrated in the story of the woman and her extraordinary cabasset find, however, this is no impediment to making a fortune.

Armor: Antique armor provides interesting insight into history and the social conditions of the times. As someone whose curiosity is jogged by antiques, I have often wondered why it was that during the Crusader times the Knights (i.e. the rich landlords) were so heavily armored and the lowly foot soldiers (i.e. the farming peasants) were lightly protected, only to have this change in later periods when the officers wore silk finery and feather hats and the foot soldiers carried the metal. Were the early knights braver, and therefore did more fighting in their heavy chain mail and armor? Or did they get smarter and just sit back directing in later wars?

I know, I know. Being the cynic you are, you're going to tell me that in both cases the officers stayed back so that they wouldn't get hurt and that it was the grunt foot soldier that took the brunt of the fighting!

Antique body armor has a language all of its own. Almost all of it came from Europe, including that worn by the Spanish conquistadors that invaded the Americas. Helmets (cabassets), visored helmets (bascinets), cuirasses (breastplates), cuisses (shoulder armor) and crinet (horse armor) are just some of the descriptive words used. Full body sets obviously cost more, like an Italian circa 1600 composite-etched, full foot armor, including bascinet, for around $10,000.

Of all the individual armor pieces, helmets are the favorite. If you purchase other body armor, make sure all pieces come with it for maximum value. If you can find antique pieces with the leather padding or protection still in good condition this increases the value of the item considerably.

Tip: Don't polish body armor, even if it is really grungy. Better to wash it in warm soapy water and lightly oil with very fine machine oil. Let it sit for an hour and then wipe it down with a soft cloth. Some rust and aging gives armor character and makes it look more authentic.

A fun antique, body armor can often be associated with specific battles such as the conquistador campaigns in Mexico. Pieces with such a provenance are much in demand.

Crossbows: Antique crossbows are difficult to find. If you can locate an 18th century Flemish crossbow with windlass and original string it is worth around $3,000. A late 17th century German one with detachable steel bow and six bolts goes for about $8,000. Unfortunately, not many antique crossbows come onto the market.

Daggers: Scottish Highlander daggers, Bowie sheaths and blades, and SAS (Special Air Services) daggers of all sorts are highly sought after. Japanese WWII bayonets and American stainless steel fighting knives with leather ring handles made by Camillas of New York, are a few of the others. But it is the German Third Reich daggers that are the highest priced and the biggest segment of the antique dagger market.

Hitler's Third Reich looked upon the dagger not just as a hand to hand fighting tool but also as a power and status symbol. It is for this reason, as well as for the infamy of the SS, that their daggers fetch the highest prices of more than $1,000. If you can find one for sale, that is. Daggers with inscriptions on the blades made by Robert Klaas and by Alcoso Solingen often fetch even more.

Right behind these SS daggers come those of the Luftwaffe, the Wehrmacht, and the WWII Kreigsmarine (Navy). Bayonets for the same German military services are also popular among collectors, although not as much.

Scottish, Celtic, and pre-15th century historic daggers are sought by museums but do not reach the high prices of items from the Third Reich and the German Imperial period. If you ever get a chance to go to London, go into the London Museum and see the collection of Stone and Bronze age daggers they have displayed. It is fascinating what our ancestors did with mere flint.

Recommendation: Definitely a collectors market, daggers are not mainstream antique items. They do, however, have a very active, collector's sector.

Swords: Japanese WWII swords followed by Napoleonic hussars and Scottish basket hilted swords are typical of this category. No pitting and no rusting, matching blade and scabbard numbers, and hilt and handle in good condition distinguish higher priced Shin-gunto swords. Rarity also means increased value. While an average imperial Japanese Sword is valued at around $500, the upper end of the market is represented by such pieces as a circa 1861 gold and jewel mounted sword valued at over $150,000. This particular sword was presented by Prince Michael Obrenovitch of Serbia to Prince Alexander Couza of Moldovia.

Asian swords and 18th century Indo Persian swords, while rarities in the United States, often come on the market in Europe. Called Shamshirs, the highly decorated swords with a history are worth five-figure prices. Given as gifts among royalty, they were not just fighting tools but also works of art. A gold and diamond encrusted Shamshir, mounted in two colors of gold and presented by Abdul-Medjid, Sultan of Turkey, to Prince Alexander Couza, is typical. The hilt is encased in gold, encrusted with patterns of rose diamonds, and chased with foliage, while the leather covered wooden scabbard is decorated en suite with gold mounts. What is unusual about this sword is its gold bullion knot attached to the hilt. Valued at $30,000, it will be worth three times that when fully restored.

Swords, like daggers, are collector's items and the market price is governed by rarity and demand. The fancier the hilt basket the higher the price obtained for these historical antiques.

Blunderbusses, sporting guns and pistols: Genuine blunderbusses with their distinctive bell-shaped barrels are difficult to find and replicas cloud the market. The only real way to tell the difference is to get a provenance with the purchase of such items as many blunderbusses have distinctive Georgian or early Victorian manufacturer markings that can be traced back to specific owners. A rare segment of militaria, they are valued around the $3,000 mark at 1998 prices.

Sporting guns: This small class of antique firearms consists of sporting pistols, usually in pairs such as those by German manufacturer Jacob Kuchenreuter. These are often distinguished by their blue octagonal barrels and their brass bound oak cases. Even rarer percussion or flintlock long barreled rifles also fit into this class. The more modern but considerably more expensive, sporting shotguns from renowned manufacturers such as Holland and Holland are not generally classified in the antique market as they are considered more of the top echelon of the modern day sporting gun.

Flintlocks: American-made flintlock rifles and muskets are extremely popular antiques and command good prices. Typical of this class would be the model 1803 U.S. Flintlock rifle made by Harpers Ferry Armory of Virginia around 1814 to 1820. With its 54-caliber, single-shot muzzle loader, 36-inch part octagonal, part round barrel, and brass patchbox on the right side of the half stock butt, this would be on the market for approximately $3,500.

Springfield Armory late 1800s models in good condition are also sought after. Flintlock "Kentucky" rifles going even further back are often embellished with silver inlay and these rare pieces are definitely collector's items.

Pistols: Flintlock firing mechanisms identify antique pistols, many of which are considered works of art due to their ornate silver decorations. French, German, Spanish, British and American flintlock pistols made by manufacturers such as Alden Thurber & Co., of Worcester, Mass., fill this class of antique firearms, which enjoys a brisk turnover. Pairs of dueling pistols, often beautifully decorated, complete with embossed leather cases, are much sought after and many antique gun dealers specialize in these pistols alone.

Pistols can be considered the apex of the antique firearm business and prices vary from reasonable to beyond $50,000. This is a very specialized business and this antique class needs expert knowledge. Eighteenth century pistols by J&W Wood, England, Piraube Aux Galleries, Paris, and M.C. Pistor Cassel of Germany are names that are commonly known in the trade and are much desired.

Revolvers: Colt London Models 1849 revolvers inscribed Col. Colt London, complete with cases and cleaning tools, are the type of revolver popular with serious collectors. So are unusual revolvers, such as a five-shot, .31 caliber percussion pocket revolver, manufactured and stamped by Bacon Mfg. Co., of Norwich, Conn.

Russian officer's baton.

As with all antiques, revolvers are a window into history and no history is more exciting than that of the West. The Colt Walker revolver is a great example of what was produced at that time.

First produced from specifications drawn by Capt. Samuel Walker of the First United States Mounted Dragoons, only 1100 were manufactured in 1847 for Walker's A to D cavalry companies. With satin finish, one-piece walnut grips, and case-hardened, blued, 9-inch, .44 caliber round barrel, they weighed a hefty 4-1/2 pounds and were considered horse pistols rather than holster revolvers. But it is the revolver's long, 15-1/2 inch length that conjures up the image of a Dragoon officer standing proudly on a hilltop overlooking Gettysburg. By 1860 the army had replaced most of the original Colt Walker's with Model 1860 army revolvers, which were the major Civil War sidearm.

The 1851 Navy, which was also stamped Colt London on the barrel, was a smaller version of the original Colt Walker, and it was this 2-3/4 pound, 14-inch barreled gun that tamed the Western frontier when it became the revolver of choice for cattlemen, scouts, lawmen and rustlers alike.

Truly the gun that tamed the West, and the various Colt models are identifiable based on various historic events. This is what makes revolver collecting so fascinating for the vast majority of enthusiasts.

Medals, medallions, orders, decorations and related items: U.S. Purple Hearts, Bronze Stars, and various combat medals jostle with German SS Close Combat badges, Afrika Corps sun helmet insignias and British Crimean War Victoria Crosses in this most crowded of antique categories.

It would be impossible to cover the medals and decorations of the world's history, yet one should never underestimate the sacrifices that the recipients of the various medals made for their countries. While the Medal of Honor, the Victoria Cross, and the Legion of Honor recognized the most heroic people, all the medals that an antique dealer handles represent considerable sacrifice. This is sometimes easily forgotten in the business.

More than any other antique item, medals and insignia are a record of historical events, some famous and some infamous. Among antique collectors, it is the ones with the most mystique that generate the most demand and therefore the highest prices. An antique beginner will find this category fascinating and the story of one medal illustrates this above all others.

Militaria offers variety.

Without a doubt the Iron Cross is the most recognized military decoration in the world. The very sight of its malevolent, matte black iron core surrounded by the dull shine of its silver frame has fascinated collectors and laymen alike. Striking a delicate balance between classic beauty and raw militarism, this phoenix among martial awards resurrected itself four times over two centuries following the Prussian War in 1813. Rising again in 1870 during the Franco-Prussian war, in 1914, at the onset of WWI, and again during the Third Reich in 1939, the Iron Cross epitomized raw military power and Adolf Hitler's concept of world domination.

On Sept. 1, 1939, on the very eve of the Second World War, Adolf Hitler signed the Great Renewal Order that reinstated the dispersal of the Iron Cross for the last time. Radically altered in appearance from the earlier, Schinkel-designed Iron Crosses, the new Nazi cross was larger and had the swastika as its central theme. It is these infamous versions of the Iron Cross, encased in an award box, that are collectors' prized items. When one peruses the turbulent history of this medal through four wars, one can fully understand why medals hold such a fascination for most people.

Orders, and insignia and campaign medals are the bread and butter of the militaria antique business. With an almost inexhaustible supply of items coming to market, specialized militaria antique dealers abound in malls and on cities' main streets. Almost exclusively a male preserve, these antiques are such a huge category that a beginner interested in them will find no shortage of products available.

Before leaving medals alone I want to give you an idea of how much money some medals sell for.

In May 1998, a posthumously awarded Victoria Cross came up for auction in London where it sold for a record 138,000 pounds ($220,000). Awarded to Flying Officer Lloyd Trigg, a New Zealand Royal Air Force pilot, it sparked memories of a heroic episode from the Second World War. The unusual thing about this Victoria Cross is that it was awarded solely on the testimony of the German U-boat commander whose marauding submarine was sunk off West Africa. Despite his bomber being crippled by the U-boat's fire, Flying Officer Trigg pressed ahead with a suicidal low level attack that sunk the submarine. Details of the heroism displayed came through the evidence given by the captured U-boat commander himself and it was solely on his testimony that Flying Officer Trigg was awarded the Cross.

Now isn't that story worth the $220,000 paid for the medal?

Recommendation: Unless an amateur really loves antique medals and insignia, I would not recommend them. It is a crowded market with experts abounding. If you do feel that strongly, go for it!

Headdresses: Military headdresses form a small part of the antique business but a few are worth mentioning for the mere fact they're interesting. Prussian metal helmets circa 1850 are recognizable by their spikes and gilt metal chin straps. German steel helmets from both World Wars are another item that is available. But it is the Imperial German Guard Cuirassier helmet with tombac skull, leather-backed brass chin strap and winged-eagle crest worth around $5,000 that is top of the pile.

The most interesting headdress that I have seen for sale was an Irish Horse Guard's bearskin with a St. Patrick's blue feather plume, velvet-backed graduated-link gilt chin chain, and leather lining. At $800 in a London antique store, it looked magnificent and was worth every penny of the price being asked.

Uniforms: Uniforms, like headdresses, are specialists' collector's items. Apache and other Indian buckskin jerkins, and beaded waistcoats could also be considered uniforms. So can Indian scout moccasins and leather water containers. Although difficult to find, these Western memorabilia are sure to increase in value dramatically.

Miscellaneous militaria: As with most antique categories, miscellaneous military items abound. Brass Chinese cannons, German hunting swords and German etched halberds are just a few. All have a market, albeit a small collector's one. That is what is so exciting about the whole antique business. Everything fits into some category, no matter what it is.

Here are some unfamiliar words used by antique militaria dealers.

Halberd: 15th and 16th century weapon with an ax-like blade and steel spike mounted on the end of a long shaft. What one would call a "forceful persuader!"

Glaive: A sword, especially a broadsword.

Sporran: A leather or fur pouch worn by Scottish Highlanders at the front of the kilt.

Gimp: A narrow band of cord or braid used for trimmings.

Trousse: Personal possessions.

Pelisse: A long outer cloak often worn by military officers.

Pepperbox: A container with small holes in the top for powder.

Percussion: The striking together of two bodies.

Gorgets: Armor protecting the throat.

Shamshire: A Persian curved sword. Not a scimitar, as the blade is evenly sized.

Recommendation: Since militaria antiques are a specialist market I would recommend the following:

> $1,500 and less — Percussion revolvers, gorgets and shoulder badges such as the Luftwaffe parachute badge.

> $1,500 to $5,000 — Revolvers, Japanese swords and better quality shotguns is my recommendation.

> $5,000 and more — I would suggest complete suits of armor, Medals of Honor and the Iron Cross.

Summary

Militaria antiques are difficult for anyone besides the enthusiast. The market is small and prices are very much controlled by knowledgeable people. I know some people will disagree considering how huge gun shows are, but if you relate the number of gun enthusiasts to how many people buy antique furniture for their homes, you will appreciate what I mean. Don't forget the old sales maxim: The larger the retail market, the easier it is to get a slice of it.

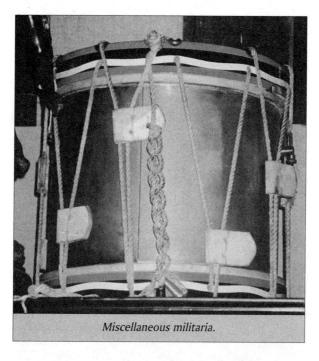

Miscellaneous militaria.

Chapter Twelve

Collectibles

Collectible items are loosely classified under categories such as "Blue Willow."

As defined in the dictionary, the word collectible means an item collected as a hobby or for purposes of study. While I agree with this strict interpretation, I would have added "for pleasure" to the definition, particularly as it pertains to antiques.

The antique world is full of collectible items and these are loosely classified under categories such as Blue Willow, Ephemera, or Antiquities. Many of them diffuse into a number of different segments. Ceramic plates are just such an example, as plates can fall into commemorative, Blue Willow, Staffordshire and many other loosely termed collecting definitions. Whenever one's hobby is discussed, however, one word is always constant. It's the word "pleasure."

Bearing that in mind, this chapter will be fun because no other items bring as much pleasure to the public at large as collectible antiques. I'll begin with an entertaining story of the origination of the Blue Willow pattern.

Legend has it, there once lived a wealthy Chinese Mandarin called Chao Cong who had a beautiful daughter named Hong Shee. Being his eldest, she was the apple of his eye and Chao Cong made plans for her to marry a wealthy business partner's son, both to consolidate their businesses and because he felt that his friend's firstborn would make his daughter happy. Unfortunately, Hong Shee was already in love with her father's secretary, a man named Chang.

On learning of her affection for Chang, Chao Cong fell into a rage and imprisoned his daughter in the palace while banishing his secretary Chang back to Sinkiang Province where, isolated and in shame, he could have no contact with Hong Shee.

The legend of the Blue Willow.

Later that night, while black, rolling clouds covered the full moon, Hong Shee escaped and met Chang by the lake where the two lovers embraced before hurrying over the bridge to a waiting boat.

Unfortunately for Hong Shee, her father was unable to sleep and while smoking his pipe on the parapet he spied the two lovers and gave chase.

But he was too late. Having reached the boat, Chang cast off and as Hong Shee sadly watched the figure of her father recede into the night, they set sail across the lake with only a prayer to the gods to guide them.

Unfortunately for the lovers a storm developed, and being only a secretary with no nautical knowledge, Chang was unable to maintain steerage on the boat and it capsized under the weight of a huge wave, drowning both lovers still clinging to each other as they went down.

The legend of blue willow is that as the father watched from the shore he saw two brilliantly white love birds appear and float gently to heaven. In memory of this, Chao Cong instructed his factory to imprint this scene on all his palace's pottery.

Two hundred years ago blue willow first gained popularity in England and that popularity has not faded with time or lifestyle changes as so many things do. It is as collectible today as it ever was and antique blue willow is highly prized wherever antiques are collected.

Of interest to the antique collector is that the blue willow pattern is found on many types of antique ceramics produced by all the major manufacturers such as Royal Doulton, Staffordshire, Wedgwood, etc. True Blue Willow always has the picture of Hong Shee and Chang crossing the bridge pursued by Chao Cong. If you see blue willow without the three figures, it's just another fake, of which there are many.

Recommendation: Blue willow will continue to gain popularity. It is now one of the leading patterns in home decoration, and antique blue willow pattern ceramics of all makes as well as tapestries and tablecloths will continue to appreciate. Original pieces of Chinese porcelain are obviously the most desirable.

Toby jugs: Toby jugs are so called after Toby Philpot, the subject of a popular song published in 1761. The original Toby jug was made by a well known potter called Harry Elwes and the English Wood family pottery produced them as early as 1715, well before the song popularized them. The popularity of Toby Jugs with collectors is due to the variety of funny characters that are available. This led to the production of many "character" jugs, the difference being that the "character jug" is just a head and shoulders caricature while the Toby jug is a full figure mug.

Minton, Doulton, Walton and Wilkinson Ltd., all made Toby Jugs as did just about every pottery in England. A great collectible, Toby Jugs attract both male and female collectors worldwide.

Recommendation: Toby jugs will continue to grow in popularity. An antiquer should aim to find jugs by the more obscure manufacturers such as A. Neale and Co., England. Their 1795 creamware jug of a jovial man holding a mug of frothing ale sells for over $1,500 and their other jugs also fetch the highest prices. If interested in this pottery, I suggest that you join one of the many Toby jug societies and get regular newsletters updating you on this specialized collecting segment.

Perfume bottles: One only has to think of Jesus in the manger in Bethlehem being visited by the three wise men carrying gold, frankincense, and myrrh to realize how far back the history of the perfume bottle goes. Collecting antique perfume bottles has increased tenfold in the last few years with a commensurate increase in prices. The reason is that they make great conversation pieces as well as interesting items for curio cabinets.

When collecting perfume bottles, anything goes. No particular manufacture or period of manufacture matters — as long as the bottles are old. Glass perfume bottles, porcelain ones, hand-carved wooden ones, and intricate metal ones are all desirable. Since they come from all the corners of the world, they all have a story to tell.

Perfume bottles come as straight bottles with daubers or as the more modern atomizers. All are collectible but it is the antique dauber bottles that are most sought after. Unusual ones such as the small

Perfume bottles are increasingly difficult to find.

necklace bottles strung on a leather thong to hang around the neck or the sterling silver ones manufactured in the late 1800s encrusted with semi-precious stones are valued in the $1,000 plus bracket. Gold Victorian ones are worth even more.

For the antique collector, perfume bottles are incredibly worthwhile. Manufactured throughout the ages in all corners of the world, perfume bottles come in every material imaginable. Wood, silver, brass, glass and gold — anything goes. Most are of individual design and as such are instantly in demand by collectors.

Recommendation: Now increasingly difficult to find, perfume bottles are still an antiquer's dream with interesting products continuously being discovered. Prices are forever rising and will continue to do so.

Teapots: Teapots, from the 1770 Chinese family rose teapots to the 1930s sterling silver ones, are a big antique segment. Many collectors love them and specialize in specific makes such as Minton, Wedgewood, or the William Greatbach factory. Styles vary from plain design blue willow or Flow Blue to character teapots that depict tree

Many collectors love teapots.

Many beautiful spoon collections are handed down from mothers to daughters.

trunks or nursery scenes. Even historic records are depicted on silver or ceramic ones.
Recommendation: Teapots are an excellent collector's antique and vary in price from $100 to $5,000.

Spoons: Many beautiful and interesting spoon collections are left by mothers to their daughters. They're mainly of silver, but ceramic spoons are also part of this collectible category. Hung in a black velvet lined case they make a great display. Tiffany and Gorham 1860s spoons are popular and many enameled ones are worth about $300 each.
Recommendation: Stick with themes when collecting antique spoons. For instance, choose spoons that commemorate a certain city, or that depict an African-American theme. Sets of spoons are more valuable than a whole mix of different ones.

Pens: Parker, Mont Blanc, Mabie Todd, lacquered Dunhills, and Conway-Stewart pens are increasingly sought by collectors in an antique category that has gained tremendous popularity recently. Valued from around $200 to more than $2,000 for a lacquered Dunhill pyramid-shaped pencil with an ocean ship with full sail design, pens are both a practical and collectible antique.

The history of the word pen as defined by Webster's dictionary is interesting. Derived from the Latin "penna," which originally only meant feather, the first known pen was the reed pen, or calamus, used to apply ink to parchment. In time the reed pen was replaced by the sharpened and split feather called penna, or "feather used to write with." The Latin "penna" then changed to "penne" in French, only to be hijacked by the English who shortened it to "pen."
Recommendation: A great collectible that is growing and highly profitable, pen and pencil sets are the ones to go for as are gold or gold-plated ones. Condition is everything as repairs are next to impossible, especially on the nibs.

Antique tiles: Tiles are a new, and fun, collectible. Delft blue and white tiles depicting religious stories dominate this class although red transfer print is also popular. Dating back to the early 1700s, antique tiles are a "sleeper," fast becoming a hot collectible.

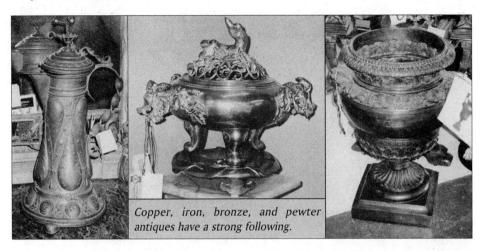

Copper, iron, bronze, and pewter antiques have a strong following.

The stories depicted on them are terrific conversation pieces and collections of same-set tiles fetch up to $1,000 for a set of six.

Recommendation: Tiles are highly recommended. Condition, once again, is everything. Go for the delft.

Cameras: Most often collected by men, cameras have been around for a long time and are a surpassingly large antique category considering one doesn't hear much about them. In London, I have even seen full-sized stores selling nothing but antique Leitz, Eastman Kodak, Zeiss, Leica, Hassleblad and Nikon cameras, many at prices approaching $10,000. Some of the names such as Newman and Guardia, Voigtlander Bijou, Stegemann-Berlin, and W. Kunik are only known to specialists in this category, which also covers lenses, plates, advertisement objects and documentation. In America the 1920s Graflex large format speed camera even has a society dedicated to its history.

Speaking of history, the first cameras used pinhole technology and were made from sea shells, coconut shells, and even wooden Pagoda models. Recorded in Chinese texts from the fifth century B.C., it was the Chinese that discovered that light travels in straight lines.

The philosopher Mo Ti was the first to record an inverted image with a pinhole or screen. In the fourth century B.C., in the western hemisphere Aristotle asked, "Why is it that when light shines through the fingers of both hands when crossed to form a sieve it appears circular in the form of a cone?" Not till the 16th century did the Arab physicist Ibn Al-Haitam finally theorize the linearity of light — the basic principle in camera technology.

The history of cameras could fill a book but credit for the first picture goes to Gemma Frisius, an astronomer, who took that photograph in 1545. The word "camera" comes from the words "camera obscura," which means "dark room" and was coined by Johannes Kepler (1571-1630).

Recommendation: If cameras are your thing — go for it. Antique cameras are bound to increase in price in this electronic age and they have a large following. That aside, they are fun to tinker with and are wonders of light refraction technology. They can also generate good profits and make wonderful den decorations.

A good bet, copper antiques are always in demand.

Copper antiques — especially those from the 17th century — have been discovered by interior designers.

Copper/Iron/Pewter/Bronze antiques: Classed under a general "metalware" category, copper, iron, bronze and pewter antiques have a strong following. Not as exciting as precious metal antiques, these metalware items, especially copper, have a great following.

Copper: Recently discovered by interior decorators, copper kettles, wine coolers, coffeepots and lidded saucepans are in great demand — especially old circa 1700 ones. Priced from $100 for simple kettles to $7,000 for 30-inch wide wine coolers with gadroon decoration and paw feet, antique copper is in. Specialized booths and stores are even suddenly appearing in most antique malls. If marked Gorham & Co., prices skyrocket. A good bet, copper antiques are always in demand.

Iron: The least expensive of the "metalware" items, iron door knockers, cast iron animal models and profile relief plaques are still good items. Of course, if you find a pair of wood-mounted, cast iron torcheres sculpted with classically draped women holding torches, and stamped with the name Miroy Freres, Paris, you will be able to pay off your credit card balance with the $20,000 to $25,000 you'll definitely get at auction.

Pewter: Hidden away among metalware, pewter is a surprisingly durable category of antiques. A silver-gray alloy of tin, copper, lead and various antimony mixes, pewter was considered fine kitchen and tableware in the 17th and 18th centuries. Why they didn't get lead poisoning, I don't know. Pewter flagons are top pewter items with 1600s English James I examples demanding $3,000 at auction. Chargers (large plates), sconces, soup tureens (can you imagine the punch in that soup!), ewers and 23-inch French cisterns in the form of a dolphin with the basin formed as a scallop shell are all great pewter antiques. Pewter is an antique sleeper about to catch fire.

The "poor man's bronze," brass antiques hold their head up high.

Bronze: What comes to mind when you think of bronze besides busts, figurines, rippling muscles, torsos, hunters, and fisher boys? Throw in Joan of Arc, dancing girls, concubines, cupid and a whole host of imaginative shapes and you have an antique category with items costing anywhere from $1,000 to $1 million for a piece!

What to say about bronze except busts, rippling muscles, figurines and torsos.

Bronze antiques boggle my mind. If there is one category where the beauty of man's imagination is obvious, this is it! Study your artists, periods, styles, patinas, marble, casting techniques and a whole host of finishes and you'll do fine. Now all you have to do is decide if you can afford to dabble in these wonderful antiques! I personally love them, but then I'm only a writer and therefore an observer. Seriously, though, this is a terrific antique category since bronzes epitomize all that's beautiful in mankind's history.

Brass: A "poor man's bronze," brass antiques hold their head up high. Many dealers specialize in them exclusively, which tells me that they make money. Mixing brass and copper items has become the hot decorating trend. Middle eastern perforated serving trays are all the rage as are brass Russian samovars. With prices for brass antiques ranging from less than $100 to the mid four-figures, brass is a good antique beginner's category. Follow your nose and buy what you like and you can't go wrong in brass. No great manufacturers or periods are important — preference is what counts.

Sewing collectibles: Surprisingly, there are quite a few sewing collectibles around. Treadle and tabletop sewing machines manufactured by names like Cookson, Florence, Weir and Singer are the most common. Sewing boxes, porcelain needle cases and enameled etuis get higher prices, however, especially if they have tortoise shell or mother-of-pearl inlay.

Among the various sewing collectibles, thimbles figure prominently. Metal ones, gold and silver ones, porcelain thimbles and matching pairs of thimbles are very popular. When seen in a presentation case they are fascinating, particularly as many porcelain thimbles are commemorative versions of prominent American and European cities.

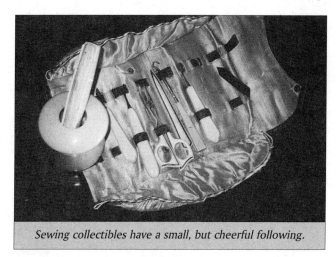

Sewing collectibles have a small, but cheerful following.

Sewing collectibles have a small but cheerful following. Prices stay steady and they are more enthusiast's collectibles than dealer items.

Fishing collectibles: Fishing reels (almost all trout or salmon reels), lures, rods and fishing knives make up this growing antique category popularized by Robert Redford and the movie "A River Runs Through It." A recent yuppie phenomenon, trout fishing collectibles almost all come with the name Hardy stamped on them. This English reel manufacturer goes back to the late 1800s and their desirable Perfect, Silex Multiplier, Uniqua and Alnwick reels are difficult to find. Not to be outdone, American manufacturers Thos. W. Chubb circa 1887, B.C. Milam & Son circa 1885, B.F. Meek circa 1880 and Wheeler and McGregor circa 1895, are also highly collectible.

And then there's the "Ultimate Collectible Rod & Reel." In 1929, Abby and Imrie, fishing tackle suppliers based in New York, NY, advertised a world famous gold rod and reel in their fishing tackle catalog. Costing $2,500 to make in 1876, this engraved solid gold reel and matching bamboo rod with gold reel seat and ferrules was first made for the Centennial Exposition in Philadelphia where it was specially featured. It was also exhibited at Chicago's World's Fair in 1893 at the specific request of the U.S. Fish Commission and again at the Paris Exposition in 1900, where it won the Gold Medal for best exhibit. Shortly thereafter it disappeared. Made of the best handmade split bamboo with solid gold mountings, the rod's butt end was encrusted with topaz stones and the reel seat and ferrules were beautifully engraved with "The Gentle Art of Angling" fishing scenes.

What a beauty! Can you imagine what that combo would be worth if you had it today? Unreal.

Lures: The first manufactured fishing lures were recorded in Izaak Walton's book "The Complete Angler" published in 1653 in England. Almost all were metal revolving lures with opposing fins that turned up and down to cause the revolving motion produced with the help of the exaggerated tails. Although gutta-percha (hard rubber) ones were occasionally mentioned as being available, there were no wooden ones in England until the Jock Scott lures made by Hardy Bros. came along.

The first commercially manufactured lures made in America came from Michigan and Ohio and were produced by Heddon and Pflueger who dominated the market from the 1900s to the 1940s. The first wooden lure was designed by accident as James Heddon was sitting alongside his favorite lake in Dowegiac, Michigan, when he tossed a piece of whittled wood into the water only to have it struck by a bass. Latching on to a good thing when he saw it, he started producing wooden lures post haste.

The first reels made in America came from Kentucky where, in the early 1800s, the jewelers Meek, Milam, Talbot and Sage were the only people with the tools and the talent to make these works of art.

For anyone interested in fishing and its evolution, fishing antiques are terrific collectibles. Still a growing segment, these antiques are sure to appreciate in value. At prices ranging from $100 to an average $500 they are worthwhile collectibles.

Musical instruments: The Stradivarius violin must be the best known of all antiques. Its million dollar value makes it so. There are other violins such as the Italian ones by Andrea Guarneri and Enrico Rocca that are valued at around $60,000 however.

Antique musical instruments include grand pianos, brass wind instruments and even circa 1900 "Standard" gramophones, and it is these that most musical instrument collectors go for. Even musical boxes and pin barrel organs can be classified as musical antiques and these are the items that are priced within reach of the average collector. Among American musical antiques the guitar, squeeze box (accordion) and drums figure prominently.

Antique harps are wonderful antiques that never age. Irish-made ones such as the walnut and giltwood harps by Jackson of Dublin with their eight foot pedals and beautiful harmonica curves are very reasonable at around $2,000.

Ten-key boxwood oboes with onion and cotton reel finials, brass keys and the Brille key are another instrument that is sought after as are many ethnic whistles, tambourines, calypso drums and violin bows.

A large class of specialized collectibles, musical instruments offer their owners hours of playing pleasure. I would recommend that when collecting musical antiques you stick to one instrument type. An expensive category, collecting musical instruments is not for everyone.

I would also like to add a few words about jukeboxes. Expensive, but highly collectible, working jukeboxes are always in demand. Ranging from $2,000 to more than the cost of a car, jukeboxes are the nouveau riches' idea of home decoration. I approve as long as they are in the game room and not the living room.

Boxes/Tins: Tea caddies, knife boxes, smokers' boxes, biscuit boxes, snuff boxes, trinket boxes — the list goes on and on in collectible boxes. And before you ask why tea caddies have become such a big collectible in the last few years, I'll tell you — nobody else knows, either! They certainly don't get used for storing tea. Maybe it's because the mahogany, rosewood, harewood, fruitwood, ebony, burr yew and tortoiseshell boxes are so pretty. Or the fact that tea as a beverage has become very popular with the population at large.

If you are in to collecting boxes or tins you are dealing with a winning collectible. This antique segment is growing like wildfire and tea caddies are getting so difficult to find that prices of rare ones are reaching $5,000. As with most English furniture, tea

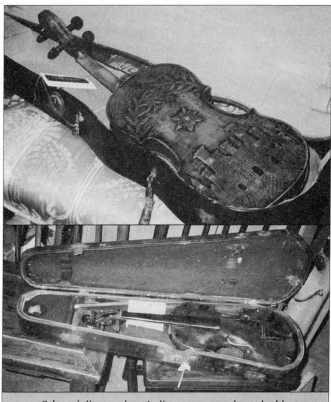

Other violins, such as Italian ones, are also valuable.

Collecting musical instruments is an expensive category, and is not for everyone.

caddies are classified by the Georgian, Regency, Queen Anne and Victorian periods. As before, condition is vital for price appreciation. A beginner should ensure that a tea caddy's legs are there if it originally came with them. These get broken and dealers often remove the others rather than repairing the broken one.

How do you tell if the caddy had legs? By checking the corners, my dear. If the wood coloring is lighter in the four corners you can bet your bottom dollar that the antique originally had legs. If they're gone, knock the dealer's price down by 30 percent. The caddy is simply not complete!

Snuff boxes make very colorful collectibles. Mother-of-pearl, silver embossed, enameled and rococo gold decoration was all used on 18th and 19th century snuff boxes, which were considered as much an article of jewelry as they were a carrying box.

Antique storage tins are another fast growing segment, especially recently. They must be in perfect condition, however, as damaged ones, unless very rare, are not popular. Decorative tins depicting old Victorian street scenes and country scenes are most in demand but there is a growing trend in collecting coffee, tea, and baking powder tins. Lady Hellen coffee tins retail for up to $100 and Sanka, Yuban, and Sanborn tins sell for around $30. Davis Baking Powder, Tetley Orange Pekoe tea and old Hershey's Cocoa tins are also wanted.

Antique boxes and tins have enough interest in them to satisfy most collector's tastes. Ranging from expensive snuff boxes encrusted with precious stones to interesting cocoa tins for a few dollars, antique boxes are fun. If interested in trading rather than collecting, I would suggest you stick to tea caddies and snuff boxes.

Leather goods: Antique leather goods encompass the whole gamut from metal cabin trunks to small traveling bags. Louis Vuitton fitted dressing cases for both male and female travelers are in demand at around $4,000 but this antique category even covers doctor's instrument bags at under $100. A very specialized antique category, leather goods are in demand as much for what's inside them as for the carrying case itself.

Fans: Fan collections are quite rare. Cantonese, Japanese, German, French and Victorian English fans painted and lacquered with classical scenes of gardens are the top standard in this surprising category. I say surprising because would you believe that rare fans such as a 1775 silk leaf French fan with mother-of-pearl carved sticks and cherry picker design change hands for as much as $5,000?

Collectible fans are little-known in the general antique business, but I predict that this won't be for long. If you are a beginner in antique collecting, I would suggest that this might be a category for you. Fans can still be found at very reasonable prices mainly due to the fact that demand, while growing, is still low — an ideal antique situation.

Plate collecting: Antique plate collecting is big business, so much so that large stores selling nothing but collectible plates can be found in most towns and cities. Commemorative, limited issue, portrait, and rare individual plates from almost every porcelain and ceramic manufacturer throughout history fit the definition of "collectible" in this class.

This is huge. So huge in fact that it would be far more useful for me to explain some of the specific things to look for in collecting plates, rather than advising you which ones I recommend. That will depend on your own interests and personality.

If you are in to collecting boxes or tins, you are in to a winning collectible.

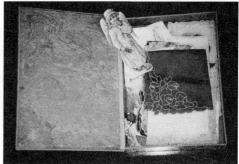

Antique boxes have enough interest in them to satisfy most collectors' tastes.

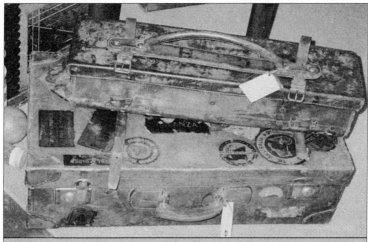

Antique leather goods encompass the whole gamut, from trunks to traveling bags.

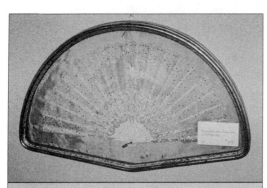

Collectible fans are obscure among antiquers — but not for long.

There are so many plates in the market that it's easy to get carried away.

Plate collecting is big business.

Here are a few things plate collectors should bear in mind:

Commemorative: A plate created to mark a special date, holiday, or person. It does not mean limited issue.

Issue price: The original price upon introduction of a plate, established by the manufacturer.

Open-ended series: A collection whose issues appear at intervals, usually biannually or annually, with no limit to the number of years in which they will be produced and no up-front explanation of the total number of issues in the series.

Limited edition: Applies to any item produced with a specific number of pieces in the line — usually anywhere from 250 to 10,000 pieces. This practice became popular in the 1960s. The success of limited edition plates depends on the reputation of the firm, the artist or designer, fine craftsmanship, and a strictly numbered edition with the number on the plate and a certificate of authenticity.

As I mentioned at the beginning, antique plates are big business and give collectors both pleasure and profit. I would definitely recommend that the beginner start collecting antique plates, but would also recommend that you concentrate on one line. There are so many plates in the market that it is easy to get carried away. Just remember — same type or design collections make far more money than a hodgepodge of different types.

A collectible bible — where does one start in such an interesting category?

I recommend 18th century pewter.

In closing out antique collectibles, here are some commonly used words and phrases.

Etui: A small, unusual ornament.

Antimony: A metallic element used in alloys.

Gadroon: A band of convex molding ornamentally carved with beading or reeding.

Ironstone: Various kinds of iron ore mixed with silica and clay. A hard white porcelain.

Woodblock transfer: A woodcut depiction.

Polychrome delft: A piece of pottery decorated in many versions of blue.

Frits: A vitreous substance used in making porcelain or glazes.

Pique: A tightly woven fabric with various patterns of weaves, produced especially by a double warp.

Wrigglework print: A writhing pattern.

Flagon: A large vessel with a handle and lid for wine or ale.

Socle: A plain, square block higher than a plinth serving as a pedestal for a sculpture.

Recommendations: Where does one start in such an interesting category? So many collectibles with so many interesting items make it difficult to recommend any particular purchases but there are some basic rules to follow, depending on whether you are in the antique business for profit or for pleasure. If for pleasure, buy what you like first and foremost. It's for your own enjoyment after, all.

When buying collectibles for profit I would recommend that you stay with the most popular categories: blue willow, perfume bottles, plates and carriage clocks come to mind immediately. It is these antiques that are most in demand and as such, the demand drives up prices. Since antiques have a limited supply, prices continue to rise ensuring your continuing profits.

$1,500 and less — I recommend beginners look at 18th century pewter, percussion pistols, aeronautical memorabilia, blue willow and delft.

$1,500 to $5,000 — 17th century pewter, blue willow, delft, English shotguns, rare rods and reels, Georgian and Japanese swords and rare medals are what to go for.

$5,000 and more — What else but rare blue willow? Also, bronzes by well-known sculptors, Rolex watches, cased pairs of shotguns and, if you can find it, the "ultimate rod and reel" collectible.

Summary

No single antique category raises more emotions, expectations, or gives such pleasure to so many people as the collectible category. If you don't believe me just go to an antique mall and talk to a few dealers selling Blue Willow. And other categories are no better. Some people could argue the merits of the Walker Colt or Remington rifle for an entire afternoon.

Collectibles are the lifeblood of the antiques business — the "hormones" I like to say. In the next chapter I will discuss architectural antiques for one main reason. It is the fastest growing retail segment of the antique business, bar none.

No single category raises more emotions, expectations, or gives such pleasure to so many people as the collectible category.

Collectibles are the lifeblood of the antique business — the "hormones" I like to say.

Chapter Thirteen

Fountains, Garden Furniture, Pedestals and Finials

Architectural antiques are the fastest-growing segment of the antique business.

Architectural antiques are the fastest growing segment of the antique business. Many of the products are used for both exterior property enhancement and as chic interior decoration. Wrought iron gates, metal foot scrapers, marble statues, fireplace fenders, garden tables, benches, fountains, and urns make this category a long overlooked, but increasingly sought after antique category.

But what exactly is an architectural antique?

Broadly speaking, architectural antiques consist of two categories — that which is salvaged, such as paving stones, balustrades, or roof tiles — and that which is manmade, such as statues, garden ornaments and chimney pieces.

Many dealers claim it is not possible to fake bronze, but that's not true.

Before I cover the various products that comprise architectural antiques, I will discuss the materials used in these products, which will enable you to establish that what you are buying is in fact antique. As is usual with an antique category that suddenly becomes hot, fakes are appearing posthaste. Here are the materials most commonly used in architectural antiques and their distinguishing characteristics.

Lead: It is very difficult to distinguish between new lead and antique lead after a few years of exposure and some judicious waxing. The lead items produced in the 18th century were of very high quality and the intricate detail is clearly distinguishable, which cannot be said of the modern fakes. This is the single most noticeable feature between antique and fake lead products. Specifically: Fingers in fake pieces are often fat and blurred, hair is a blob, instead of clearly defined strands and faces are expressionless. Size is another giveaway. Antique lead figures were full sized, whereas fakes are clearly smaller to save material. "Three-quarter" size is what I call it.

Bronze: Many dealers claim that it is not possible to fake bronze but this is incorrect. Modern chemicals and metal compositions in the hands of expert fakers changed that, and they produce perfect copies of antique originals complete with green patination. The only way to tell if it is a fake is in the reputation of the seller, in the cleanliness of the underside of the product, in the wear in patination caused by handling, and, most importantly, gut feeling. If it's too cheap, it's probably a fake. Don't forget that signatures and foundry marks are easy to reproduce and that they are no guarantee of originality.

Cast iron: The easiest metal to reproduce, cast iron antiques can nevertheless be identified by their weight. If it isn't heavy as hell it's probably a fake aluminum mixture. Garden ornaments and furniture produced in the old days also had the small casting marks removed. They could do it in those days, labor costs being what they were.

Limestone and sandstone were the most commonly used material in the old days.

The most highly prized and now virtually unobtainable marble is of a creamy white color with no veining.

Secondary marble, or Carrara, has considerable veining but wears well because of its hardness.

Nowadays it would cost too much to have someone de-burring everything. Blurred detail is another giveaway in fakes as far eastern factories produce hundreds of items out of the same molds. This tends to wear away the delineation. As with bronze, foundry marks mean little.

Stone: Limestone and sandstone were the most commonly used materials in the old days. Limestone was preferred for statuary and sandstone for architectural features although it tends to turn a dark black and green color as it weathers. Sandstone is also harder and so details are clearly visible. Being more brittle it also tends to chip. Both these materials are hard to repair so if the antique is badly damaged, forget it. That is certainly true if you are purchasing the item for investment purposes. If for your pleasure you might appreciate the worn look, "distressed" is the word used today for the beaten-about look.

Marble: Antique statues used white Italian marble. The most highly prized and now virtually unobtainable was a creamy white color with no veining. Most fakes are easily identifiable because they use a brilliant white marble from India. This marble is highly crystalline and easily recognized. Secondary marble, or carrara as it is called, is bluer and has considerable veining but wears well because of its hardness. An old wives' tale is that marble can be restored if it becomes sugary. This is incorrect. Once broken down, marble is beyond restoration.

Identifying fake marble is best done by checking clarity of the carving and true proportions. The old artists were very particular about detail and ensured that arms and hair were carved away from the body. Facial expressions were also as accurate as possible. Bored or excited really meant that in the old ages!

When checking for dating, the same features as for marble apply — cleanliness, with no air holes, well delineated features, and arms standing proudly away from the body.

Terra-cotta: The color of red earth, terra-cotta has been used since pre-classical times for architectural antiques. Ideal for statuary and planters because of its weathering properties, antique terra-cotta comes in the most desirable yellow color and in the least desirable red. Antique planters, oil jars, and troughs are highly desirable for gardens, but due to the fragility of the material, few genuine items can be found.

Reconstituted stone: The poorer version, reconstituted stone antiques are very durable due to the hardness of the material. When checking for dating, the same features as for marble apply — cleanliness of material with no air holes, well delineated features, and arms and hair standing proudly away from the body. All these indicate a genuine article.

With those descriptions behind us I will now cover the various categories that make architectural antiques increasingly popular, particularly to new homeowners with a hankering for the nostalgic. Just remember that most architectural antiques are big, cumbersome, and heavy and that planning is required before purchasing. I know of people who bought a huge statue only to find that the moving costs exceeded the purchase price.

Wrought iron: Antique wrought iron gates, fences, trellises and decorative head boards are suddenly in unbelievable demand. The more intricate and complex the casting, the more desirable the products are. Used as wall decorations, trellises, gates and wrought iron section fences for climbing plants, they are being popularized by interior decorators. I even had one decorator purchase two metal fence sections from my store

Wrought iron is in unbelievable demand.

in Grapevine and make them into living room tables by adding smaller sections as legs. Once green-tinted, plate glass tops were added they looked absolutely terrific.

Obtainable at most flea markets, antique wrought iron can be bought for a few dollars from those who don't know what they have to many thousands from those who do. The genuine articles are distinguished by heavy but intricate castings, lack of over-welding, material composition and weight.

Recommendation: I never pass up buying a reasonably priced piece of wrought iron and always make a profit on it. You can, too.

Fountains: Antique fountains are so popular that a whole industry has sprung up and begun to reproduce them. Cast iron, stone, or marble, all antique fountains sell before most dealers can get them onto the floor. Genuine cast iron and Italian marble antique fountains go for a fortune and I have seen an Italian white marble with cupid and two doves sell for $9,000. Prices vary so much that I can only give you very broad guidelines of approximately $1,000 for stone fountains, $3,000 for cast iron and $5,000 for marble ones.

Bird baths: Like fountains, antique bird baths are in short supply. Cast iron ones are virtually non-existent, but carved sandstone ones can occasionally be found at prices around $1,000.

Chimney pots: I have noticed more and more English chimney pots in antique shipments coming from England. They seem to be an item that is suddenly coming into fashion and decorators use them as indoor planters. Since they come in all shapes and sizes from 24 to 48 inches high they are ideal for this purpose. Prices are still reasonable at around $150 so they are ideal for the antique beginner. Unlike the fountains and gates they also fit into most sport utility vehicles and can be transported without calling on the nearby haulage company. I would highly recommend chimney pots as they sell briskly.

Antique doors: Antique doors, particularly the all wood ones, are available at most antique malls but at four-figure prices. They can be found considerably cheaper in rural states like Wisconsin or Idaho. Stained glass doors are considered rare, unlike windows, and cost more than most people's monthly salary. Despite this, I think that antique doors combined with other smaller architectural antiques such as chimney pots make an excellent line for the antique beginner.

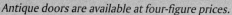
Antique doors are available at four-figure prices.

Stained glass doors are rare.

Fireplaces and surrounds: Antique fireplaces and surrounds have been extremely popular in Europe for a long time and are now catching on in the U.S. More and more of the cast iron 19th century ones are now found in antique containers shipped to the U.S. and I believe this is due to the fact that the new gas and electric heating units fit into them. Many of the cast iron fireplaces have a tile surround and these are extremely pretty. Not exactly cheap at around $800 to $1,000, cast iron fireplaces are, like the chimney pots, a coming thing in the antique business.

Fireplace mantels and surrounds have been a much sought after item in antique malls for a long time and fetch high prices. Even in Europe, a Louis XVI fireplace mantel sells for 5,000 pounds ($8,000), so only the cheaper, $1,000 units tend to make it to antique auctions in the United States. Even so, they are worth a beginner purchasing as there is a constant demand for mantels.

Fireplace fenders and chenets: Antique copper fireplace fenders and brass chenets are popular. Highly intricate figurine chenets and those with mystical themes, such as a sphinx with female faces and breasts, sell for more than $3,000, but any antique mall has the more familiar dog, cat, and animal ones for around as little as $100. A good addition, antique fenders and chenets are regular sellers.

Antique garden furniture: An extremely popular category, genuine cast iron antique benches, garden seats, stools and tables are in short supply. Most of the ones you see in stores are aluminum replicas from Mexico. As a result, prices for highly

A good addition, antique fenders are regular sellers.

Pedestals, posts, and finials.

decorative genuine pieces reach more than $5,000, particularly as these are now used for interior sun rooms, patios, and even living rooms. I would not recommend this category to the beginner as genuine antique garden furniture is hard to find and mistakes are easily made.

Antique wooden furniture is also popular and, unlike the cast iron pieces, relatively available. Prices are reasonable and with supply plentiful the prices for rustic benches and tables is fairly stagnant.

Very occasionally I have seen antique Italian marble garden furniture but the prices were so high that I would not recommend tying up your capital in such expensive units.

Pedestals, posts and finials: Mainly decorative, antique pedestals and finials suffer from the fact that they are so heavy. Marble or stone lions and gargoyles are the ones that are in demand but smaller French urn designs and Corinthian styled plinths also sell. A fringe item, antique pedestals and finials are best left to the established dealers.

Statues: Antique statues are often found in the gardens of historic homes or in those of wealthy personalities. Most are marble, but terra-cotta and sandstone works are seen occasionally. Requiring considerable finance and sufficiently large gardens, statues are not an everyday antique product. Best left to the experts, statues are nevertheless a reminder of more genteel times. Among the designs, statues of Eros or a winged cupid predominate, followed fast by naked buxom ladies which, rather than looking erotic, appear extremely graceful. As an afterthought — maybe it's the shy downward looking faces and contented looks on such statues that does it!

Marble, sandstone, and terra-cotta predominate in statues followed closely by bronze. Expensive to buy and move, statues are not a beginner's antique.

Troughs and planters: With the rise in popularity of rustic antiques, troughs and planters came into their own. Desired for their "country" look, antique planters are now used more for interior decoration than for exterior planting. Made of lead, marble, stone and cast iron, antique planters are great items for your home or for

With the rise in popularity of rustic antiques, troughs and planters came into their own.

Like planters, urns are now used as interior accessories.

resale. With a steady supply available, prices for such antiques vary from a few hundred dollars to many thousands, depending on material used, age of the planter, and complexity of design.

Antique urns: Like planters and troughs, urns are now used as interior accessories. Smaller in size than planters, they are easier to handle and are subject to brisk bidding when they come up for auction. Cast iron urns are very popular but marble, stone and reconstituted stone all sell well. They vary in price from around $500 to many thousands of dollars for white marble, and are increasingly in demand. Highly recommended, antique urns will continue to appreciate, especially Italian marble ones with complex designs.

Antique stained glass windows: A few years ago no one wanted them but now you can hardly find one. It seems that the public suddenly discovered stained glass and with it, antique stained glass windows took off. The problem is that supply is limited and because of this, prices have gone through the roof. I like stained glass windows, especially those with coats of arms, flower portraits, or Christian scenes. If found, such windows will set you back anywhere from $500 upwards. And that's for a small one. One thing to remember: If the paint on the wooden surrounds is peeling don't repaint them. People like the authentic look and feel it illustrates the fact the window came from a church or old building. One other thing: If you ever see a round framed stained glass window for sale, buy it. Very few of these ever come on the market anymore. Antique stained glass windows are good buys and I highly recommend that if you find any you purchase them for your own pleasure or for profit.

Antique stained glass windows are good buys.

Garden bronzes: As can be expected, garden bronzes are expensive. A set of late 19th century Japanese bronze cranes, for example, will cost around $5,000, and a pair of French cast bronze children with ram's horns costs twice that. Higher end antique stores find that they do really well with bronze garden antiques and I believe that this trend will continue.

Sundials: What a wonderful antique! Sundials are seldom found, but when you do find them, they are terrific products to buy. Many antique sundials are stone with bronze indicator rings and are used both in the garden and on an open porch. Unfortunately for both the antique collectors and the dealer, they are few and far between. To give you an idea how rare they are: A 39-inch Georgian sundial recently sold at auction for $4,800. If you ever see one and you can afford to purchase it, do so. You'll definitely have many hours of pleasure from it or make a hefty profit if you resell it.

Antique baths: Isn't it funny how things come around again? A few years ago people were tearing antique baths out of their bathrooms and installing the modern fiberglass or expensive porcelain ones. "Ugh, they're so old fashioned," they said, turning their noses up at that high-sided antique tub.

Now it's practically impossible to find one to buy. I personally believe that it's got to do with them being used in torrid movie love scenes, such as the one in "The Bridges of Madison County." What woman wouldn't want to be rubbing Clint Eastwood's back in a bathtub?

Antique copper bathtubs sell for up to $5,000 and the porcelain ones with four claw legs for a little less. If you can find the giant brass taps to go with them, you've got yourself a winner! When considering an antique bathtub try to get one with the highest sides you can, particularly at the back. Not only are they worth more but they also make you feel like a movie star!

One of the most interesting antique bathtubs I ever saw was in a dealer's yard in Bristol, England. It cost 6,000 pounds ($10,000). An 1890 seven and a half-foot long stoneware bath with a beautiful mahogany surround, it surprisingly had a mahogany encased thunder box attached to it up by the head of the tub. When I first saw it I wondered if people were less inhibited in the 18th century until I realized that because it was encased, the thunder box was more likely used as a seat for the lover as he washed his beautiful mistress' back. Oh, well! It's the romantic in me, you know.

Antique wash basins are also in demand, although not as much as bathtubs. Pretty porcelain ones with flower patterns go down well, as do the old marble scalloped ones. Priced at between $500 and $1,000, these are also going up in price. Just don't forget that both the bathtubs and the basins should be in first class condition, although you can get away with just a few dents on the tub. One or two chips make it look more authentic. I did say one or two.

Miscellaneous architectural brick-a-brack: Just before writing this paragraph I spoke to an antique dealer friend of mine who asked what I was writing about. When I told her it was "architectural antiques" she got very excited and told me that she was thinking of specializing in them in view of all the excitement being generated by this newly discovered category.

Weather vanes are very popular.

"But is there enough variety?" she queried.

"Is there enough variety in architectural antiques?" What a question from a dealer!

Time to look at some of the different products.

Gazebos: If you can find them, antique gazebos are worth a fortune. Unfortunately they seldom come up for sale. Expect to pay up to $15,000 for a good wrought iron one.

Old water pumps: As decorator items they make great conversation pieces. They can be frequently found for around $500.

Postboxes: The cast iron type sell rapidly if you ever find a genuine one. Hardware stores are full of replicas that were made in Mexico, but genuine ones are very scarce.

Antique safes: Wonderful items, safes sell well. They are expensive, however, and you can expect to pay more than $1,000 for a big, heavy one. The problem is moving it.

Heating radiators: Antique radiators are more popular on the East Coast than in the rest of the country and have a very small collector following. Inexpensive, they are used more for decorative purposes.

Weather vanes: Very popular, antique weather vanes are few and far between. 1930s aluminum, copper or bronze weather vanes fetch around $3,000 for good examples.

Bricks: Antique bricks? Yes. Not so much in the United States but in Europe and the Far East. Here is a story that might interest you.

When I used to buy and ship container loads of antiques from Europe to the U.S. I had a number of wholesalers that I always bought from. One of them in Wales had a permanent pile of old antique bricks in one corner of his three warehouses. I thought they were just rubbish. One day I saw him loading them into a container and asked him about them.

"Oh, I've got this Japanese client who buys them all," he said. "In Japan they build wooden houses and real, natural stone bricks are impossible to find. My client always insists that I fill the bottom of the container with them as she sells them like hot cakes."

The other reason that antique bricks sell well in Europe is that building laws stipulate that when rebuilding or adding on to your property, you have to use the same material as the original. Can you imagine hunting for such bricks if the antique wholesalers didn't have them? How on earth would one ever repair an old cottage?

Staddle stones: Before you think that I've really lost my mind, let me tell you that you are unlikely to ever find a staddle stone antique in your neck of the woods. Staddle stones are 18th and 19th century English stones that look like mushrooms. Around 30 inches high, they were used as a base for propping up the first layer of hay or straw bales. Staddle, in fact, means just that — a foundation or base for stacking hay.

Staddle stones are popular as garden antiques in England and Europe as they look like a mushroom out of a fairy tale. Just imagine a fairy sitting on such a stone mushroom and looking at you quizzically!

That wraps up architectural antiques. Here are a few words that are not so well known.

Fifteen-hundred dollars and less — I would advise you look for antique planters.

Chenets: Pairs of fireplace ornamental figures.

Sarcophagus: A stone coffin.

Mortar: Either or a vessel in which substances are crushed, or a mixture of lime, sand and water.

Royal warrant: A Royal authorization. Usually a certificate.

Roundel: A curved form or panel often found on antique gates as a central feature.

Andiron: One of a pair of metal supports for fireplace logs.

Convolvulus pattern: Several trailing or twining plant patterns found in casting designs.

Trefoil base: Three-legged bases. Used when describing fire iron stands.

Putto or Putti: Cherubic, angelic baby boy or boys described as such on Italian marble statues.

Recommendations: Its difficult to recommend any one item over another in architectural antiques because they are all so popular and will continue to be so. I personally think that all are good.

> $1,500 and less — I would advise you look for antique planters. They always sell well and who wouldn't want a beautiful plant or flower display in her home? Especially if it is a great verdigris-green antique iron planter! Fireplace chenets also fall into this category.

> $1,500 to $5,000 — The fountain, birdbath or garden bench has to be the choice. They really are treasures if you can find them.

> $5,000 and more — I have to go with the cast and wrought iron gates. Who doesn't want these as an entry piece to their home or as a trellis decoration in the house with climbing plants all over them? Expensive fountains, particularly cast iron ones, would be my second choice in this category. Now all you have to do is go for it!

Summary

Architectural antiques can best be summarized into two categories — architectural salvage and architectural antiques. Items such as bricks, balustrading and chimney pots can be classified as salvage; iron gates, benches and statues as antiques. Whichever sub-category they fit into, however, architectural antiques are the hottest thing since sliced bread.

Despite this, architectural antiques are a difficult category for the beginner or collector. Very little information exists and the category is being inundated with fakes. The best advice I can give you is the same as before. Deal only with a long established, reputable dealer who will refund your money should what you buy turn out to be fake. Another word of advice is "Buy what you like!" First because you can live happily with your purchases, and secondly, because you are unlikely to be misled by fads.

As with all antiques, you get what you pay for in architectural antiques. That very delightful cast bronze 19th century birdbath is not going to come cheap, but it will certainly appreciate in value far quicker than the chipped and repaired stone one. As with all reasonable buys, with a little luck it will give you a healthy return on your investment in a short period of time.

Architectural antiques are the hottest thing since sliced bread.

There are four main choices when purchasing architectural antiques: At the auctions, from general antique dealers, at flea markets and at specialist dealers. The argument for the specialist is that they know, or should know, what is fake and what is not. At flea markets you are more than likely to be ripped off with no recourse so I would avoid this if possible. It's amazing how antique that "Made in Mexico" fence section can look after a week in the dirt and rain. The argument in favor of buying at a general antique dealer is that sometimes they don't know what they have and you can pick up a bargain.

The little old lady with the antique booth in a small town antique mall is not always prepared to research a piece of what, to her, looks like old iron. Especially since, like most dealers, she runs an antique booth mainly for enjoyment and not necessarily for profit.

When purchasing expensive architectural antiques such as marble statues, I recommend that you only deal with the professionals. Ask for a detailed receipt giving full disclosure of the date of manufacture, material, previous ownership and/or appraisal. Full provenance records are also what you should try for.

In concluding this chapter I would urge an antique beginner to look at architectural antiques. If you can overcome the transport, handling, and lack of information details, they will give you great pleasure and considerable return on investment.

The next chapter is full of general information for the beginner that I believe you will find useful.

If you can overcome the hardship of transportation and handling they will give you great pleasure.

Chapter Fourteen

Tips, Terms and Miscellaneous

What to buy?

When I first got involved with antiques I spent months wandering through antique malls, observing hundreds of auctions, and reading everything that I could lay my hands on. To my surprise, I found that this exciting and highly diverse industry, so full of history and rich tradition, was peopled by dealers who knew little about it and even less about making money in it. Studying it further I realized that this was due to the incredible growth of the antique malls, which allowed individuals with little or no retail training to become proud owners of their own antique businesses. Even years later, after running my own successful importing business, antique wholesale warehouse, and a high-end retail store, the situation hadn't changed. The result was my best selling book *Money From Antiques* followed by the even more successful *More Money From Antiques*. For those readers who have not read them, I would recommend you do so, not so much because I would make more money from royalties but because as a beginner you should know how a dealer operates to get the best deal for yourself. Knowing how auctions are organized will also further your chances of picking up a bargain, and even more important, of not losing your shirt!

This chapter on "tips and terms" will give you some basics that I have found invaluable during my own antique career.

What to buy?

As antiques beginners continue to get more involved, they should ask themselves why they are doing so. Is it because they have an interest in historic items and they like the idea of antiques? Is it because they like them for personal use? Or is it because they want to make some money and trading in antiques sounds as if that is possible? No matter what the reason, the following should always be born in mind.

1. Buy what you like. That way at least it will give you pleasure.
2. Never believe that just because it's an antique it must be valuable and cost a lot. This is a favorite of dealers who try to hoodwink you by saying: "Of course its not cheap, it's a genuine antique!"
3. Realize that different antique product lines have different buyer groupings. Antique furniture, for example, has a general retail audience and as such is bought by up to 70 percent of the population. On the other hand, collectibles such as wartime memorabilia have a very limited buying audience and since these items are purchased with disposable income, war collectibles do not appreciate as much as accessory antique tables. One reason architectural antiques are so hot right now is that mortgage interests are low

Buy what you like. That way at least it will give you pleasure.

If you are not absolutely sure, go away and sleep on it.

When you do see a bargain, grab it.

and many people are becoming first-time homeowners. The first thing they do is decorate their new home and, since baby boomers like eclectic things, they buy wrought iron gates with climbing plants and use them as decoration. By the way, an indoor vine on a wrought iron gate fixed to the wall looks absolutely marvelous!

4. If you are not absolutely sure that you are doing the right thing when making a purchase go away and sleep on it. The item will still be there tomorrow, I guarantee it. Don't wait too long, but don't rush either.

5. If unsure about a price, go away. Then ask around or hurry to the nearest Barnes and Noble and check the value of an equivalent piece in the reference books.

6. If you are getting into antiques for the money, stick to the types of items that have a large buying public — furniture, mirrors, watches, jewelry and antique planters are obvious examples.

7. Never pay what the dealer or seller first asks. Unlike the general retail business, antique dealers expect you to bargain. Don't feel ashamed of doing this. It's part of the business and adds fun.

8. When you really do see a bargain, grab it. If it's genuine it won't be around for long, that's for sure.

9. Watch out for the details. As I discussed in previous chapters, antiques are established as being so by provenance. The discolored glue in the joints, the clear lady's hair strands in the iron planter molding, the illegible signature on an old Blue Willow plate and the sterling silver identification that you can hardly see because it's buried among the ivy engraving — these signs all tell you that the antique is genuine.

10. Have fun. If you don't, you'll end up hating the antique business for its inconsistencies, its often belligerent dealers, its lack of clearly defined parameters, and its general lack of discipline.

If you do all of the above, the antique business will give you more fun than any other business that I know of. What could be more exciting than to find that the old parchment that looks like it should be thrown into the garbage can is actually covered with Picasso's doodles and that you can now retire? Which brings me to the three cardinal rules that govern collecting antiques for profit or for pleasure.

If you can display your antiques, they will be a daily source of enjoyment.

Art Pottery: ornamental ware either hand-decorated by artists or glazed with special effects.

For Pleasure:
1. Entertainment — If it pleases you, it'll be fun.
2. History — If it has a history, it'll be interesting.
3. Display — If you can display your antiques or use them, they will be a daily source of enjoyment.

For Profit:
1. Demand — A large buyer market ensures sales turnover and therefore profit.
2. Rarity — Governs the demand which guarantees profit. The more rare the item is, the more profit you can make.
3. Condition — The better the condition, the better the return.

Dealers all know these cardinal rules. They also know and bandy about many terms and phrases as if they know what they mean. I'll give you a few so that you get the idea that they're really used to try to befuddle you. It's fun when you hear them used. Just don't take them seriously. I'm also adding a few tips to save you money.

Ceramics

Art Pottery: Ornamental ware either hand-decorated by artists or glazed with special, controlled effects. In other words, pottery made and decorated by hand.

Backstamp: The information contained on the bottom of a piece of porcelain or pottery. It can include item name, designer/artist signature, identification number, date of copyright, manufacturer's logo and artists' markings that identify when it was produced.

Casual china: Porcelain dinnerware that is thicker, heavier, and more durable than fine china.

Bisque ware: Clay that has been hardened through a first firing. Bisque firing is the first firing or baking in high heat.

Never strip or refinish a piece of furniture if you think it has some value.

One of the mistakes beginners make when cleaning an old or dirty piece of porcelain is that they wash it with hot water while rubbing with a soft cloth. This has the effect of breaking away tiny pieces of the gilt or glaze with the dirt. It is far better to let the piece soak in liquid soap and warm water overnight before gently letting the stream of tap water take off the grunge.

Another tip is that you should never try to touch up a pattern that is damaged. Better leave it as it is. Once you touch up on top of the glaze no one will be interested in the piece.

Furniture

Never strip or refinish a piece of furniture if you think it has some value. Rather, you should wax it with a beeswax (carnauba) that soaks in. Quickly buff it and do it again until the patina comes up with that deep luster that is the hallmark of good antique furniture. Clear beeswax both feeds the wood and cleans it. Many people use lemon oil which makes it glisten. This is a real no-no. It instantly devalues the piece. What if you

Never polish silver antiques until they are shiny clean. Better to leave the crannies dark — it gives it character.

New categories are continually springing up.

have a chair with a leg that's loose? It is better just to squeeze in some neutral colored space-age wood glue than to try to take them off to redo them, which could result in something breaking. In any case, a little bit of a wobble indicates a genuine antique. Beside which, it only takes a few minutes to squeeze a dollop of glue but hours to remove and re-fit the legs.

A bureau with brass handles and escutcheons: This means that it has brass handles and a shield or shield-shaped emblem bearing a coat of arms as an ornamental plate for the keyhole.

Carved armchair with scrolling arms on baluster supports: An armchair with carved arms dipped in the middle on supports in the form of an elongated bottle.

Windsor armchair with turned splayed legs joined by crinoline stretchers: Armchair with legs joined by coarse, stiff fabric or horsehair.

Lowboy with herringbone inlay on cabriole legs: A low table-like chest of drawers with a pattern made up of short slanted lines on outwardly carved legs that narrow down into an ornamental foot. Popular on Queen Anne or Chippendale furniture.

Oyster veneered and marquetry chest: Oyster patterned veneer (thin layer of wood used to cover inferior material) and alternate wood or ivory inlayed chest.

Silver

Never polish silver antiques until they are shiny clean. Better to leave the corners and crannies dark because that's what gives antique silver its character. If the piece is really dirty it should be soaked in warm water, liquid soap, and lemon juice. Do not leave the silver in the water for long periods as the solder tends to loosen from the combination of warm water, detergent, and heat. When the dirt is loose, rinse off with cold water, rub the large areas gently with a soft cloth to give it a patina and you're done.

Who knows, they may even lead to an introduction to your favorite late-night TV host.

Tip: If repairing broken silver, take it to a jeweler and request that real silver solder be used. An expert repairer will ensure that the solder does not spill over and you won't tell the difference. A bad repair will simply devalue the article.

A George V breadbasket raised on four acanthus leaf, cabochon and C-scroll feet: A breadbasket on four large, thistle-like, leaf design, shiny, convex cut, C-shaped feet.

Victorian quatrafoil-pierced cake basket: A Victorian era-made basket in a four-petal flower or four-lobed leaf design.

A George II toilet box cover with engraved coat of arms: Can you imagine having a silver toilet box cover with your own coat of arms engraved on it?

Chamber candlestick: These are small candlesticks that come with a base plate, carrying handle, and a conical extinguishing tool. They were used to light your way through dark corridors rather than leaving the candle in one place.

Silver epergne: A silver container with a central bowl and attached smaller baskets on extended arms. They were used to serve cookies or sweets.

Sterling silver hallmarks indicate town, period, and material composition. Many price guide books have these listed for American, English, and French silver and I would recommend that you get yourself one if you are serious about collecting silver.

Miscellaneous

By now I am sure that you will have realized that the antique business is forever evolving and that new categories of antiques are constantly springing up. That's the fun part of the business because you, as a beginner, can be as much an expert as the next dealer in these new product lines. Here are some items that are gaining popularity.

Equestrian antiques: Antique saddles, bridles, bits, and halters are a fast growing segment of the antique business. These items are not just collected by horse lovers but by interior decorators working on 'rustic' decorated eateries.

Antique cars: Who hasn't heard about multi-million dollar car collections owned by entertainment personalities like Seinfeld and Jay Leno? What a wonderful thing it must be to be able to afford such a pleasurable collecting hobby! But that doesn't mean you can't be involved. How about collecting badges (emblems), old car paintings, literature and even rare photographs? These are all part of car collecting, and who knows, they may even lead to an introduction to your favorite late night TV host!

Typewriters: Antique typewriters are very collectible and will become even more so as the computer age continues to drive the writing business. A German Picht type wheel model Braille typewriter with bell, roller inker, and Braille letter index is already worth over $7,000 and rising rapidly. Incidentally, Oscar Picht produced a number of specialized typewriters and shorthand typewriters from 1899. And if you think that $7,000 is high, how about the $19,000 paid for a 1890 Swiss Velograph typewriter on a mahogany base with the circular index printing upper and lower case letters? Typewriter antiques are fun and make great conversation pieces.

Artists' antiques: A new one, artists' easels, color sticks and model limbs, faces, and bodies are becoming antiques. As more old brushes, palettes, and tools used by master painters and artists come to light, I believe that this category will gain tremendous popularity. Can you just imagine how the value of a Monet masterpiece would increase if the artist's brushes and palette with dried paint on it could be supplied with the painting?

Hand tools: Another fast growing antique category, hand tools are already standard auction items. Planes, saws, mahogany chests full of tools and many other items are now desirable. Watch out for really unusual pieces and you could do well on antique tools.

Antique dresses: Princess Diana's dresses sold for a fortune at an over-subscribed auction recently. They join a whole host of dresses, mainly by Christian Dior, Elizabeth Arden, and Sophie Gimbel that are emerging as a collectible category in their own right. Expect this to continue with prices for an average 1954 Christian Dior tulle ball gown already reaching $15,000. Princess Di's dresses reached $100,000, but this was an exception which will become the rule in the future.

Hats, boots, shoes, and purses fill out this category.

Hats, boots, shoes and purses fill out this category and interest in such items is growing. Even parasols and shawls are joined by odd antique items like throws, female lawyer wigs, and American Indian seed bag bandoleers. Children's antique clothes are also creeping into this category. A 17th century christening set consisting of bonnet, bib, a pair of mittens, linen appliqué dress, two headbands and two spare sleeves sold for $1,500 recently.

Very seldom heard of but quietly growing, antique textiles come in sections, bales, and small pieces.

Used as wall hangings, these types of fabrics are worth finding.

Kitchenalia: Yet another fast growing category, kitchenalia items, such as Queen Anne nutcrackers, already sell for $1,500. A pair of boxwood circa 1600 stylized nutcrackers in the form of a Bishop's head with bird and animal carved legends even got $3,700 at auction. Towel rails, scales, spoon racks, salt boxes, and antique knives are expanding this interesting segment of the collectible world.

Papier-mâché: Who ever heard of papier-mâché collectibles? I hadn't, but I know about them now! Papier-mâché pencil boxes, snuff boxes, food tins and even papier-mâché lacquered tilt-top tables fill this collectible category, and much of it is very pretty.

Art Deco collectibles: This is a very low-key but persistent antique category. Even as an expert I sometimes wonder why it doesn't just merge into others but for some reason it doesn't. Mainly consisting of statues, lamps, and metalware, it nevertheless throws up some interesting objects such as a plated, metal smoker's companion (tool). It's shaped in the form of an airplane and consists of two cigarette cases, four ashtrays and a cigar cutter. Merely ten inches wide, this antique combination is a wonder to behold. It could slip into smokers' collectibles, but for some reason it insists on staying in the Art Deco category.

Smokers' antiques: What can I say? Who would have thought that cigars would become such a widespread trend. Blame it on Arnold Schwarzenegger, Bruce Willis, John Travolta and a whole host of terrific superstars. The result: One of the fastest growing antique categories with cigar cutters, old lighters, humidors and rare cigars costing

Lace, quilts, embroidery, and crochet have a huge following.

hundreds, even thousands, of dollars. And it hasn't stopped yet. I am now seeing smoker's stores springing up that deal exclusively in antique items. We even have one in my hometown of Grapevine, Texas. I would, however, caution the antique beginner not to get involved too deeply. I have a sneaking suspicion that smokers' antiques might just peak and then settle back down to a more steady pace. Don't get caught at the peak.

Textiles: Very seldom heard of but quietly growing, antique textiles come in sections, bales, and small pieces. Some even sell for up to $9,000, like a 44-inch wide, five foot piece of 1893 woven silk on cotton, with repeating design of roundels enclosing classical human figures, for example. Surrounded by other designs representing the four seasons, it is very beautiful. Used more as wall hangings, these types of fabrics are worth finding. And who says that the antique business can't be innovative?

Lace, quilt, embroidery and crochet antiques also have a huge following. It almost seems as if these categories of antiques are masters of their own destiny and I expect some, like quilts, already are. A fun category for ladies, I think that an antique beginner could do worse than look at fabrics and textiles.

Ivory, jade and agate antiques: Overcome your aversion to the hunting of endangered animals, and ivory antiques definitely have staying power. They're mainly Chinese and consist of statues, animal replicas, birds, and even beer stein covers. Unless it's a very complex and large piece, prices have fallen recently. I don't expect them to stay down for long, however. Agate and particularly jade antique prices are holding steady. Plaques and figurines lead the way in agate sales.

Cloisonné and enamel antiques: Holding their own is what can best be said for these antiques. Vases and condiment dishes are popular at prices from $500 to $1,500. My own personal opinion? I don't think that this class of antiques will change much.

Guards' lamps, enamel name signs, and railway relics make up railway, or "Bring Your Work Home" collectibles.

Art paintings are a highly specialized area.

Antique billiard tables: Unsure of whether it should fall under furniture or sports antiques, old billiard tables, either way, are much in demand. Condition is paramount to attaining the $10,000 plus prices that are being reached and I expect demand for billiard tables to continue rising.

Transport antiques: Bicycles, snow sleds, dog carts, gypsy caravans and horse drawn landaus make this an interesting antique category. Depending on size and item, the prices vary, but surprisingly the horse drawn landaus at over $20,000 don't hang around long waiting for a buyer.

Wood-carved antiques: From 12 inches to 5 feet high, woodcarvings come from the U.S., Germany, Italy and England. Statues of Indian chiefs, Christian saints, the Virgin Mother and Child and carved royal coats of arms are worth up to $10,000. Carved wooden candlesticks, such as a pair of Tyrol 16th century polychrome and giltwood angel candlesticks resting on their knees, make even more. This pair fetched $24,000 at auction. The important thing to remember with antique carvings is that they should be of excellent quality and have an excellent provenance.

From the few examples I have detailed above you can see how widespread and diverse the antiques business is. It seems that every day brings a new line of collectibles which either grow or fade into a small collectible line of interest to only a very few. Some of these are worth mentioning, however, as they may take off. One of them is what are called "Work Collectibles" or as I like to call them the "Bring Your Work Home" collectibles. "Bring Your Work Home" collectibles consist of work-related items such as keys (locksmiths), firemen's regalia (helmets, axes, and bells), police collectibles

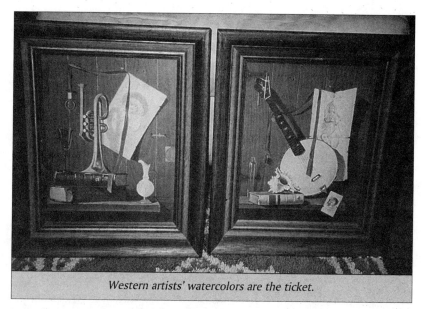

Western artists' watercolors are the ticket.

(handcuffs, whistles, truncheons, and badges), laundry antiques (flat irons, stands, heating pokers etc.), WWII U.S.A.F. and R.A.F. memorabilia, pharmacists' collections (pestles and mortars, scales, syrup bottles, etc.) and railway memorabilia (guards' lamps, enamel name signs and railway relics).

Artwork

In considering the previous chapters I am sure that you have noticed that art paintings are conspicuous by their absence. That's because it is a highly specialized area and even the experts hold differing opinions. And that's not all. Art and art antiques are such a huge category that personal choice comes into play even more than in many other antiques categories. Does one deal in Western art, Old Masters, prints or even cartoons? Take your pick, and depending on trends, you will either be blessed or sorry.

Since this is a guidebook, I am going to stick my neck out and make some recommendations. These are based on what happened in 1998 in the art business and I suggest that you treat them as a layman's guide. The choices I recommend are not made up of expensive Old Masters but of cheaper products. Here they are:

$1,500 and less — Decorative 19th and 20th century oils by lesser known painters, Old Master drawings without attribution (therefore cheap), Victorian watercolors and Western artist watercolors are the ticket.

$1,500 to $10,000 — Academic Old Master sketches and signed works by lesser known artists, good quality watercolors of Western themes, bird, animal life and farming oils, prints by the "Big Four" masters such as Picasso, Chagall, Miro and Matisse. Also American contemporary prints.

I suggest prints by well known artists.

$10,000 and more — European viewpoint paintings of North and South America, major Andy Warhol paintings, early 19th century watercolors by major artists, and fresh oil paintings by better known contemporary artists which are bound to rise over time as supply decreases.

While discussing antique art, I would like to mention that this market is very dependent on the Far East and all signs are that this area will continue to suffer financial setbacks for some time to come. This is bound to affect art heavily and other expensive antiques to a lesser extent. The American market simply won't pick up enough of the slack if the Japanese, Indonesian, and Chinese financial meltdown continues. I expect really expensive art will hold its own, but that middle priced works will suffer.

Tip: You will notice in my recommendations that I suggested originals by lesser-known artists and prints by the well-known ones. Prices of art will dip slightly but will be the first category to rise when a turnaround occurs.

Approaching the end of this chapter, here are a few more unusual words used in these miscellaneous collectibles categories.

Coalbrookdale: A 19th century English manufacturer of cast iron garden furniture and railway equipment. More famous for their iron bridges, Coalbrookdale Victorian garden furniture is very intricate and sets the standard in such antiques.

Anthemion pattern: A motif used in Greek art having a pattern of honeysuckle and palm leaves in radiating clusters.

Bacchus: Often depicted in statues and works of art, Bacchus is the mythical god of grape-growing, wine, and revelry.

Monopodium: This word is used when discussing long items and means "with a single stem."

A Dolman cape: A long, outer woman's cape named after a Turkish robe.

Lappet: A decorative flap or loose fold on a headdress or garment.

Allegorical figures of charity: Figures pertaining to the act of charity.

Epicycloidal tool: A tool that prescribes a curve dictated by a point on the circumference of a circle as it rolls on the outside of the circumference of a fixed circle. (Really! Is there really an antique tool that even does that?)

Recommendations: Miscellaneous collectibles are so diverse, so interesting, and so weird sometimes that it is difficult to recommend anything. My suggestion is that you go for what "tickles your fancy." For the beginner interested in making money from antiques I would suggest two things: First, buy my *Money From Antiques* and *More Money From Antiques* books, and secondly, take a good hard look at artists' antiques. I can't help feeling that if you found Picasso's actual brushes and palettes with old dried paint still on them they would be worth a fortune. That's what antiques are all about. Find something that has history and interest and its value is bound to increase. Lady Di's dresses are like that, aren't they?

Summary

As mentioned earlier, miscellaneous antiques cover a whole multitude of items that most of us never even think about. Enjoy them, or even better, make up a category for yourself.

You never know — it might just catch on.

Miscellaneous antiques cover a whole multitude of items that most of us never even think about.

Chapter Fifteen

Time To Take Stock

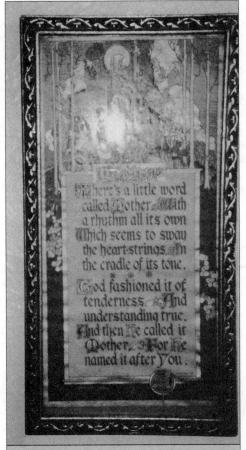

The antiques business is a living, breathing entity that's continually evolving.

We've come to the last chapter and I hope this book has been as much fun for you to read as it has been for me to write. Before I close I would like to give you some pointers that have been invaluable to me and that have made my antiques career successful.

There are thousands and thousands of antique experts, but not one of them knows it all. They never will. The reason? The antique business is a living, breathing entity that's continually evolving. What is today's trend becomes tomorrow's antique and the next century's masterpiece. The current hot fad becomes next decade's collectible, which then becomes the next century's old masterpiece. And so it goes on.

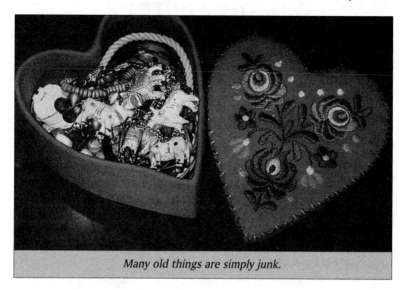

Many old things are simply junk.

This book is titled *Antiques For Amateurs.* Unlike my other books, which dealt primarily with starting and managing an antiques business, in this book I have tried to give the beginner an overall view of the fascinating, but often frustrating, world of antiques. This is important. If you sometimes feel that you can't see the forest through the trees, don't worry. The same thing happened, and still happens, to me. It's all there, though, believe me, and you will become better the more you become involved — especially after you have noted the basics I am about to detail. How one business can be so satisfying and frustrating at the same time is still hard to fathom, except if you think of it as history taking its usual twists and turns. Then it seems to make sense.

In closing out this book I would like to go over some of the basics that apply to antiques no matter what your interest is. They should always be in the forefront of your thoughts whether you are collecting for your own pleasure, for your grandchildren's inheritance, or whether you are interested in antiques purely as a profitable new business venture.

Old is not always antique

The first thing you should remember is that not everything old is an antique. Many old things are simply junk. A very few old things are antique. Whether an old item is an antique or an old piece of junk relies simply on demand. Even if the demand is small, it's still an antique. Junk you throw away, an antique you keep for its demand, which brings us to an antique amateur's fertile ground.

Most people don't know what is valuable and what is not. If you're able to distinguish the difference, you will pick up bargains at garage sales, flea markets, and even in auctions. An antique dealer I know was telling me about a ring she bought recently at a garage sale. Without any markings to indicate its age, it looked like a piece of cheap jewelry only worth the twenty-five cents the owner was asking. Knowing a little bit about antique jewelry, however, my friend realized that the delicate claw settings indicated something more. Someone had gone to a lot of effort to manufacture

Watch out for the unusual.

An antique is an object of older times with special value because of its age, work of art, or handicraft.

fancy settings just to hold cheap, colored glass! My friend took it to a jeweler and found out that what looked like gold plating was just that — and more. It was, in fact, gold plating over platinum. The glass chips were precious stones and suddenly a purchase that cost a quarter was worth over $1,800 — all because she recognized some fancy setting work! And that brings us back to the first rule of antique collecting.

Watch out for the unusual

If you look at the pictures in this book you will notice that most antiques are unusual. The curve of that Chippendale leg, the hand-painted detail on that charger, the creamy white of the Italian marble and the intriguing mechanisms of that old sewing machine are all unusual — and therefore eye-catching.

That's your first indication that the item you are looking at might be an antique. The old artisans were not just carpenters, glaziers, painters, or silversmiths, they were artists and mechanical geniuses above all else.

Just read what Webster's has to say about antiques. "An antique is an object of older times with special value because of its age, work of art, or handicraft."

It is the work of art or handicraft aspect that will help you recognize an antique even if you do not know anything about that product category.

How much should you pay?

The glib, cheeky answer would be "as little as possible," but the fact of the matter is that good, valuable antiques cost money. You can't get a rare Victorian silver teapot with a Prince of Wales provenance for a steal, and it doesn't matter what those appraisers on the fashionable antique TV shows say. Antiques like that are too well known and too valuable for them to be available for anything less than a reasonably appraised value. The best you can hope for in such a case is a small cash discount. After that you have to wait for time and appreciation, governed by influences beyond your control, to make you a profit. On the other hand, you can make a fortune on that wooden Eskimo hunting helmet that the little old lady has in her garage sale in Anchorage and that her recently deceased husband left buried in the rafters. After all, she doesn't know anything about such things, does she?

So how much should you really pay?

Well, it depends on your reason for buying. If it is for your own collecting pleasure you can pay a little over the odds (that's English for a little more). Just the hours of pleasure the antique will give you is worth that. And what is a fair price? It is the average price for such a piece that you yourself established. Perusing collectibles in the antique mall, watching the bidding in the weekly auction, and looking in reference price guides before you make a decision is all you need to do. An antique is what you, and you alone, think it is worth. By the way, treat my prices with a pinch of salt. They are average prices at the time this guide was written and with the global economy being what it is these days, they may have changed dramatically up or down.

But what if you haven't done your homework?

In that case you have to pay what the seller is asking, then forget it and enjoy the antique. No recriminations, please! You pay $20 to see a movie that only lasts two hours, so how can you be irritated about paying 30 bucks for that perfume bottle? Especially if you consider how much pleasure it will give you for many years to come. When collecting for pleasure, any reasonable price is a bargain. Just remember that and you can't go wrong.

When collecting for profit, however, the situation is completely different. For beginners, you will have to think 50 percent less. And the question you will have to ask yourself is: "Can I sell it at double the price, plus?"

Better than half-price, however, is paying almost nothing, which will probably happen only if the seller doesn't know what they have sitting on that table. Either way, you, more than the amateur collector, will have to know what you are doing, or as the English say "You 'av' to 'av' yer nyowsse about ya, mate." (You have to have your head about you, mate.)

When buying antiques for profit only two scenarios arise. The first is that you purchase a great piece with a long provenance at a touch under current prices and make 20 to 30 percent profit over a couple of years. The second is that you buy that Eskimo hunting helmet that looks like "a load of ol' rubbish" for the $20 asking price and rush out to Sotheby's or Christie's and let them auction it for $145,000. Either way, don't feel sorry for those two baby boomers manning the garage sale who forced their

When considering antiques for resale, the overriding requirement is "mint condition."

mother to sell everything and move to Chicago to live with them. It was your expertise and knowledge that enabled you to spot the bargain and it's not your responsibility to tell others their business. That is the key to being a successful antiquer — knowledge. Find it on the Internet, in the bookstores, in the malls and in the antique auctions. Find it anywhere you can.

One of the quirky things antique dealers do that always makes me laugh is illustrated by this example:

That dealer that got such a bargain on that gold plated platinum ring spent the next 20 minutes complaining that she couldn't sell a Staffordshire vase at the $480 price that a reference book said it was worth.

"I paid nearly $400 for it myself," she moaned. "You'd think that it would go just like that, even though it has a tiny repair!"

I felt like saying: "Not if it wasn't in perfectly mint condition, it won't. And certainly not when you are trying to sell it in Grapevine rather than in New York."

The point of this story is that prices vary from one part of the country to another. Even more important is the condition of the piece. That slightly damaged but repaired vase in Grapevine was only worth $350 and not the $480 mentioned in the reference book. She should have only paid $175 for it, not the $400 she did. Even if she lived in New York she shouldn't have paid more than $200. Condition is everything in the antique business.

Condition is everything

In Chapter Two I said that porcelain pieces should be in mint condition if you are purchasing them for resale. In Chapter Three I said you shouldn't clean that piece of furniture with lemon oil, whatever you do. In Chapter Fourteen I said that repairing that antique dress or hat is okay. One minute I said don't touch it, and the next I said you should. What's going on here?

When considering an antique for resale the overriding requirement is that it be in "mint condition." Smearing lemon oil on wooden furniture doesn't do that. All it does is dry out the wood and make it look fake. No antique furniture piece has that type of glisten. They have a deep glow. That only comes from nature's beeswax.

On the other hand, the condition of that dress that needs a little sewing will be improved if a seam that has a few stitches missing gets fixed. As long as the thread is of the same material (i.e. cotton rather than nylon), that is. In that case some repair will improve the condition of the dress immeasurably.

Repairs are okay as long as they are compatible and of the same material. Unfortunately porcelain, which is glazed, cannot be re-glazed. My recommendation is that, as an antique beginner, you should only deal with items in the best of condition. If it is slightly damaged it's okay as long as the antique's price is considerably reduced.

So what kind of antiques should a beginner consider?

Stick to the basics. Once you are comfortable with that, then start branching out. As a collector, follow the trends. As a buyer of antiques for profit, stay with those that have a wide following such as furniture, porcelain, and silver. The motto here is that if you can use it practically, as well for decoration, then the antique is of interest to a wide range of buyers and you have a good chance of selling it.

Is this a good time to get into antiques?

Any time is a good time for the antique business, particularly for the collector. It is a constantly evolving business filled with vitality. Having said that, it does also have its cycles, just like all businesses. These cycles depend on the general economy, but unlike other types of sales, antiques do better in a slight recession. It seems that when there is a lot of money about people drift away from antiques and when things tighten up they start buying. If you're considering going into antiques as a profitable business venture, I would suggest you start selling out of your garage before renting a space in a mall. That way, you will get comfortable before taking on lots of expensive overhead costs.

Where is the antiques business heading?

As I've reiterated in my previous books, the antique business is constantly evolving. The advent of the Internet and the worldwide marketplace that cyberspace has spawned is adding a new dimension to the antique business, as I've detailed in *More Money from Antiques*. It is also adding new headaches. While I expect this exciting new antiques frontier to keep expanding, I also expect its difficulties to continue.

Antique malls are evolving rapidly. Still the best way for a beginner to start their own antique business, a booth in a successful and heavily trafficked mall is the way to go.

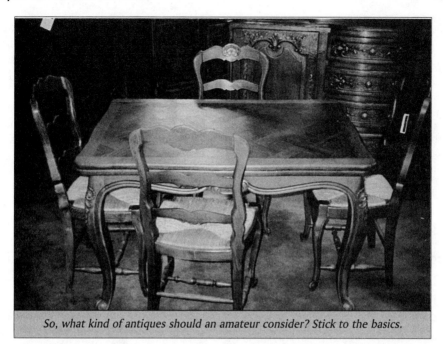

So, what kind of antiques should an amateur consider? Stick to the basics.

Take every measure to ensure that you are giving yourself the best chance possible for success. The basics detailed in Money From Antiques apply even more now than they did just two years ago. Expect antique malls to become major entertainment centers, just like general retail malls.

When surveying the antique business in the U.S. as a whole, I am always reminded that it seems to follow trends generated in Europe. That's because 90 percent of the merchandise still comes from there; therefore, it's no wonder that trends in Europe arrive in the U.S. a few years later and, as successful dealers, it is our business to anticipate these trends.

So what are the future trends?

Weekend antique fairs have caught on big in Europe, particularly in England and France. Lists and lists of these fairs are now published in magazines and local papers. Corporations are even becoming involved by taking over numerous weekend fairs in an extended area. They rent city halls, churches, and community centers, then, in turn, the organizers rent out small spaces to the individuals for a Saturday or Sunday afternoon. In my opinion this is a great development. Not only does it give an amateur antiquer a relatively cheap outlet for their products, but it also lets them get their feet wet in the business before taking on the expense of a full booth in a fixed location. I sincerely believe that this method of selling antiques will bring a whole new segment of the general population into the business.

Fairs, as described above, not only allow an amateur an easy way to sell antiques, they also open up a whole new supply market. Most of the weekend stall holders are ordinary folks who are only interested in selling the antiques they have lying

Most are ordinary folks only interested in selling antiques they have lying around their homes.

around their homes. Not knowing much about specific values, they price them for a few dollars to help pay the bills. As such, they are not aware of just how much they could get for a piece. This gives a knowledgeable beginner a great opportunity to buy low and sell high.

Weekend antique fairs are the up-and-coming thing in the U.S. and I think they will open even greater opportunities for the amateur. This window of opportunity won't last long, though. In England, professional antique dealers are already moving in on weekend fairs and acting like they are beginners to lull the buyers into complacency. Soon we will see the prices of stalls at these temporary fairs go up as the organizers realize what is happening.

But that is all still to come. The beginner should get in on the trend now as it will give him or her the experience in buying and selling before investing in a booth or full antique store.

In closing, I will make a few final recommendations that I hope will make your whole antique experience an enjoyable one.

For the interested collector I recommend:

1. If you are not sure what antiques you want to collect or buy, take your time. They've been around since 1500 B.C., and they won't disappear now. Browse the malls, talk to dealers, go to auctions and watch the TV programs. You'll soon get the hang of it and find a particular product category that interests you. And if that changes after a couple of purchases, so what? You can always sell the items and change to another line.
2. Don't take things too seriously. If you feel that the piece you are looking at is too expensive and the seller won't budge, then pass on it. There will be many more and you're not in a hurry. Collecting takes a long time. That's what the word means and what collecting is all about.
3. Having decided what you want to collect, narrow it down to a particular segment. This doesn't apply to collectibles like perfume bottles or stamps, but it does apply to wide-ranging items such as silver. Better you collect silver teapots than end up with a few plates, knives and forks, tankards, and sporting trophies. It's too messy and not at all valuable if you do it that way.
4. Finally, have fun with antiques. Laugh, smile, and sometimes gnash your teeth, but always enjoy it. In that way you will get maximum personal and professional enjoyment.

For the prospective dealer:

1. Decide what antiques you intend to deal in before you buy even one piece. Better you take your time than make a major investment only to find it's not the line you want to deal in or you don't know enough about. You can always change, but it'll probably cost you money which you can ill afford to lose at the beginning of your venture.

2. Go slowly. The biggest losses are made in the initial rush of enthusiasm. Better to take your time, make sure your first purchases are at good prices and make a small profit right from the start. Never forget that there are always other dining tables, silver teapots, toy trains, and garden planters around. You just have to find the best ones at the cheapest prices, that's all.

3. Always have fun. Nothing depresses me more than walking into an antique mall and seeing dealers who look like they're not only bored stiff, but also about to cry. Don't let that be you. You never know — the next person coming up to your booth might just buy that $5,000 buffet and then you can take the wife, husband, girlfriend, boyfriend, or partner out to dinner that night. Enjoy your success.

4. And I hope you will be successful — whether collecting for your own pleasure or starting a business. Don't forget that the advice I've given you is only part of the whole antique picture. It will, however, give you enough of an overall view that you can confidently buy and sell antiques. Just remember to have fun doing it.

Assallaam Mu Alaikum — Peace be unto you.

If you feel the piece is too expensive, pass on it.

PROFIT FROM ANTIQUE$

Money From Antiques
by Milan Vesely
A simple outline on how to profit from antiques. Turn a modest investment into a five-figure income and find out more about locating, purchasing, selling and cross-selling antiques.
Softcover ▪ 6 x 9 ▪ 208 pages
72 b&w photos
MFA ▪ $12.95

More Money From Antiques!
by Milan Vesely
You can succeed in the antiques business in the late 1990s and beyond-but only if you know how. This books will take you from the basic building blocks of owning and running a successful antiques business to some of the finer points of the business, as well as how to succeed in the ever-changing world of technology.
Softcover ▪ 6 x 9 ▪ 160 pages
30 b&w photos
MFAII ▪ $12.95

Antique Secrets
How the "Pickers" Find Treasure in Another Man's Trash
by Joe Willard
If you want to make big bucks finding frequently overlooked antiques and collectibles don't miss out on this book! Learn the skills necessary to negotiate profitable deals, how to "get there first", and determine value. Whether you are a novice seeking information on how to get started picking or a professional looking to enhance your skills the down-to-earth concepts and original anecdotes will keep you interested from start to finish.
Softcover ▪ 6 x 9 ▪ 192 pages
28 b&w photos
ANTSE ▪ $14.95

Shipping & Handling: Book Post - $3.25 1st book; $2 ea. add'l. Call for Overnight or UPS delivery rates. Foreign addresses $15 per shipment plus $5.95 per book.
Sales tax: WI res. 5.5%; IL res. 6.25%.

Dealers can call toll-free 888-457-2873 ext. 880, 8 am - 5 pm, M-F

To receive a FREE catalog or to place a credit card order,

Call 800-258-0929 Dept. MWB1

Mon-Fri, 7 a.m. - 8 p.m. ▪ Sat, 8 a.m. - 2 p.m., CST

Krause Publications ▪ Book Dept. MWB1
700 E. State Street ▪ Iola, WI 54990-0001

Or Visit and order from our secure web site: www.krause.com

SATISFACTION GUARANTEE
If for any reason you are not completely satisfied with your purchase, simply return it within 14 days and receive a full refund, less shipping.